D1397034

ONE BRIGHT SHINING PATH

Faith in the Midst of Terrorism

W. Terry Whalin
and
Chris Woehr

CROSSWAY BOOKS • WHEATON, ILLINOIS
A DIVISION OF GOOD NEWS PUBLISHERS

To the memory of

Rómulo Sauñe

and to the leaders of the Quechua church
who are carrying on his dream to plant the gospel of Jesus Christ
in the hearts of the millions who make up the Quechua nation
throughout South America

One Bright Shining Path.

Copyright © 1993 by W. Terry Whalin and Chris Woehr.

Published by Crossway Books
a division of Good News Publishers
1300 Crescent Street
Wheaton, Illinois 60187.

All rights reserved. No part of this publication may be reproduced, stored in a retrieval system or transmitted in any form by any means, electronic, mechanical, photocopy, recording, or otherwise, without the prior permission of the publisher, except as provided by USA copyright law.

Cover illustration: Chuck Gillies

Art Direction/Design: Mark Schramm

Editing: Lila Bishop

Text: 10.916/14.07 Sabon

First printing 1993

Printed in the United States of America

Library of Congress Cataloging-in-Publication Data
Whalin, Terry.
    One bright shining path : faith in the midst of terrorism / W. Terry Whalin and Chris Woehr.
        p.   cm.
    1. Sauñe, Rómulo, D. 1992. 2. Peru—Politics and government—1980- 3. Sendero Luminoso (Guerrilla group) 4. Terrorism—Peru.
5. Quechua Indians—Missions. 6. Democracy—Religious aspects—Christianity. I. Woehr, Chris. II. Title.
F3448.4.S26W43 1993   985.06'33—dc20   93-17673
ISBN 0-89107-732-4

00		99		98		97		96		95		94		93	
15	14	13	12	11	10	9	8	7	6	5	4	3	2	1

Contents

Try to imagine it. You're hiding in a cave somewhere, afraid terrorists will burst in and kill you. What gives you the strength to carry on? The Quechua people in the Andes Mountains of Peru find it in a relationship with the living God. They have access to Him through His Word in their own language.

What you hold in your hands is the story about one man from Peru, Rómulo Sauñe. God used Rómulo to give his people the whole Bible in the Ayacucho Quechua language. Throughout his work on Bible translation, Rómulo worked closely with Wycliffe missionaries. He married Donna Jackson, a Wycliffe missionary. God's Word in the language of the people gives thousands of Quechuas the strength to stand against an onslaught of evil from the Shining Path— one of the most brutal terrorist groups in this hemisphere.

We pass this book to you with the hope that you'll gain a fresh appreciation for the power of God's Word and what it can do to strengthen your relationship with the living God.

—*Your friends at Wycliffe Bible Translators*

Wycliffe
Bible Translators
P.O. Box 2727
Huntington Beach, CA 92647

Acknowledgments

Special thanks to Donna Sauñe, Fernando Quicaña, Arcangel Quicaña, Margarita and Alfredo Fajardo, Al and Barbara Shannon, Samuel Saccsara, Irma and Conrad Phelps, Richard Luna, Brenda Josee, Gaylyn R. Whalin, and many others without whom this book could not have been written.

PERU
Land of the Incas and the Shining Path

Prologue

A deep blue stretched across the seemingly endless sky. Rugged peaks of the Peruvian Andes stood like sentinels at attention. High above the tree line rose green tundra meadows, melting into patches of snow and sheets of sheer granite. Below, the golden sun washed the valleys with warmth as two bare-headed condors swooped and soared above the world in the timeless rhythm of nature at peace with itself. But for the sound of a breeze rippling across the fields of wild grass, there was only silence.

Then laughter and the sound of cowbells clanging broke the calm. With his straight black hair falling into his face, Falcon Quicaña playfully flicked his rope onto the back of a brown llama. The animal turned around and spat at the boy, and he roared with laughter.

"Race you to that curve up there," Falcon challenged his cousin Puma. "We each take a llama and drive it around the curve. The first one to get past that tree wins. Go!" With a shout and a burst of energy, the pair took off, leaving the rest of the herd in the care of a couple of small children who were servants.

Hooves clattered on the stone path as Falcon twirled his rope behind the reluctant animal. Llamas were built for carrying loads, not for racing.

"I'm winning," Falcon yelled, his brown eyes twinkling with mischief.

Driving a white llama equally in doubt about this contest, Puma Quicaña urged the animal on from behind.

Then Falcon slapped the sides of his llama and led the chase toward the flat rocks of Sacsayhuaman, a huge fortress and holy place. The massive rocks covered the entire top of the mountain to the northeast of Cuzco. When he swept around the curve at the top, Falcon let his llama head back to the rest of the herd. The animal scurried quickly away. At his heels, Puma did the same.

"Falcon, do you think we should be up here?" Puma gestured toward the ceremonial place. "Teacher Condor will be angry with us if he finds out."

"Oh, you worry too much. We're just taking a break from our studies. It's so rare that we get to see these ritual stones that we're studying all the time. We'll tell our parents that it's educational," Falcon added with a smile.

Since both boys were from the priesthood caste, they spent most of their days with the older priests, who taught them the prayers and rituals of their forefathers. The boys would one day teach these lessons to their sons and grandsons.

But today was a holiday from their studies, and Falcon had suggested to his best friend that they hike up to Sacsayhuaman. As the boys climbed the trail to the holy place, they had passed the giant stonework of their forefathers. Large rocks, four times the size of any man and equally as thick, lined the trail. Falcon marveled at the feat of engineering that had placed these rocks high above the Inca capital city. They were so tight that the blade of a knife couldn't be worked in between the blocks. Each was a perfect fit. More than decoration, the carefully crafted walls provided protection from their enemies.

At the first archway, the boys stopped to catch their breath and gaze out over the lush valleys. Field laborers dotted the patchwork of potato and *quinua* fields, part of the vast holdings of the

Inca ruler. Some of the potato fields seemed impossible to work, stretching high up the steep mountain sides. Every available plot of ground—no matter how remote—was to be worked for the harvest. Spring was planting season, and Falcon and Puma knew that the farmers were turning over the earth with their foot-plows and carefully planting the potatoes.

In the green glens that stretched like fingers curved around the rugged landscape, llamas and alpacas grazed in small herds under the watchful eyes of their shepherds. Falcon and Puma eyed the herds enviously. Though they enjoyed their privileges as future priests, they would have much preferred spending their days out in the clear air playing games while the animals grazed.

Still, they were old enough to know that a shepherd's life was not easy. From the day they learned to walk, shepherd children cared for their family's animals and hauled water from nearby rivers and creeks. They would never be allowed to spend even a single day studying the lessons of the proud Incas.

"It's beautiful, isn't it?" Falcon said with a sigh. "It's like we're on the roof of the world. I feel closer to Tayta Inti, Father Sun, up here. I wish we could come here more often."

Whump. Falcon practically jumped out of his skin. A large hand gripped his shoulder, and another hand grabbed Puma. The two boys twirled around and looked into the fierce eyes of a tall warrior.

"What are you doing here?" the warrior demanded, his wooden helmet throwing a stark shadow across his face. The bronze-skinned man wore a richly woven tunic accented with gold bracelets around his large biceps—symbols of his position as a guardian of the sacred places. "Only a few are permitted to come here. Why have you come?"

With a gulp, Falcon stammered, "It's close to the heavens and Father Sun . . . we . . . we didn't think there would be any harm in coming."

"Harm!" the warrior exclaimed. "Your presence risks displeasing Father Sun. Our crops may fail. The rains may not come. We, the royal warriors, stand as guardians of this fortress. Day and night we watch to keep this place pure and clean for Father Sun. Who are you, and why have you dared to come?"

"I'm Falcon Quicaña, and this is my cousin Puma Quicaña. We've been studying this place in our House of Learning from Teacher Condor. But we've never seen it. Today seemed perfect for a hike up here to have a look," Falcon babbled.

The warrior frowned. "Your fathers must be members of the priesthood for you to be in the House of Learning and under the instruction of Teacher Condor. You should know better. Leave now, or I'll see that you spend extra time repeating your prayers for Teacher Condor."

With that he released his grip on the boys, and they bolted toward the trail. They had run a good distance when they finally felt safe enough to slow down for a last look back. The warrior stood with his back to the sun, arms crossed, legs planted wide apart—a menacing sight. With a final glance the two boys turned and fled down the mountainside.

"That was close," Puma said breathlessly after they had put a safe distance between them and the fortress. "I'm surprised he let us go."

"We'll probably hear about it," Falcon replied mournfully as the two began to walk the rest of the way home to Cuzco along the cactus-lined path. As they approached the city, they passed caravans of llamas loaded with goods from the far corners of the Inca territory. Peasants returning from their fields nodded to each other as they hurried home. All carried themselves proudly, for they were the privileged few who lived within sight of the great Cuzco.

To the Incas and the other peoples of the Andes, Cuzco was the holiest of cities in the world, for it was the capital of their ruler, known simply as The Inca. In Quechua Cuzco literally means "Navel of the World." Together with the surrounding communities, Cuzco extended some six miles down the valley and was home to over 200,000 people. Only The Inca, his nobles, priests, and visiting chieftains with their families and servants lived in the city proper. The common people or peasantry lived on the lower side of the city.

As they passed the temple, Falcon and Puma seemed oblivious to the splendor it reflected from the afternoon sun. The *Inticancha*, or Temple of the Sun, was a part of their everyday life. But the weary traveler catching a first glimpse of the temple quickly forgot the arduous mountain journey. Inside and out, the walls were covered with gold plates, each weighing up to ten pounds. The gold was embedded with glittering emeralds and a host of other precious stones.

The western wall was emblazoned with a representation of the deity, portrayed in a humanlike form covered with gold—the sun personified. The roof of the magnificent structure was thatched with *paja*, a kind of tough grass.

Within stone outer walls stretching more than 1,300 feet stood a series of rectangular buildings—the temple itself. Here the gods and the priests made their home. Different sections were consecrated to different gods, such as the Moon God. The Moon God's chapel was similar to the Sun God's, but ornamented in silver instead of gold. The temple held three other chapels—for the host of Stars who formed the bright court of the Sister of the Sun, for the dreaded ministers of vengeance—the Thunder and the Lightning, and for the Rainbow whose multicolored arch spanned the walls of the temple with hues almost as radiant as its own.

The next day, Falcon and Puma headed into the House of Learning as the morning sun peeked over the horizon. They rushed through the door and fell onto their knees along with the other students. When Teacher Condor entered the room, the students grew silent. The white-bearded sage took his place before them, his richly decorated golden robe drawn around him with the grace of centuries-old priestly traditions.

Closing his eyes, Teacher Condor knelt before the class and, raising his arms, began to chant in a slow, lilting rhythm meant to be followed by the young trainees:

> *"Oh, Pachacamac, Creator of man, Lord.*
>   *Your servants want to see you with their feeble eyes.*
> *The sun, the moon, the day, the night,*
>   *the summer and the winter are not free.*
> *From you they receive their instructions, and you are the*
>   *one they obey.*
>   *Where and on whom have you given your shining*
>   *scepter?*
> *With a joyful mouth and a joyful tongue,*
>   *day and night will come to your call. Fasting.*
> *You will sing with the voice of the nightingale.*
>   *And perhaps in our joy, in our good fortune,*
> *from whatever corner of the world,*
>   *the Creator of man and the Lord almighty shall hear*
>   *you . . .*
> *Creator of the world on high and of the world below,*
>   *Creator of the mighty ocean,*
> *Vanquisher of all things,*
>   *where are you?*
> *Speak, come.*
>   *Truth from on high,*
> *Truth from the deep, Molder of the world,*
>   *Power over all that exists,*
> *sole Creator of man,*
>   *ten times will I worship you with my feeble eyes.*
> *What splendor! Before you will I prostrate myself.*
>   *Hear me, O Lord! Give ear to my cry, O Lord."*

The chanting droned on for hours. The rhythmic tones rode like a fragrance on the soft morning breezes into the passages extending like graceful fingers from the House of Learning. Teacher Condor would lead with a phrase, and his pupils followed in a precise rote that lifted their spirits and joined them in worship. They would repeat these chants throughout their years of training until these became as much a part of their daily lives as eating and sleeping.

As the master priest brought the chanting to a close, he rose reverently and sat down on a rough-hewn stool in front of the class. The students then quietly rose from their places onto their stools, eagerly straining to hear the sage's quiet voice.

"Today, students, our prayers for The Inca are more important than ever," he announced sadly. "I must tell you that The Inca is very ill." With a sigh, he added, "It is possible that he will soon pass on to the afterlife. You must not tell anyone of this, for no one is to know. If our enemies were to learn of his condition, they could take advantage of it and perhaps even challenge our great ruler's authority.

"But I am telling you this so that we may begin to learn the prayers reserved for special celebrations and ceremonies. Very soon we of the priestly caste will be charged with preparing the court for the crowning of our new ruler. You will participate in these ceremonies," he said sternly.

The boys whispered excitedly among themselves. A new ruler! It had been more than forty years since the ceremonies of the passing of a ruler and the crowning of another had taken place in Cuzco. What pageantry there would be!

Falcon thought of the last time he had seen the heir to The Inca. As servants carried the royal prince on a gilded litter through the streets, Falcon had stood at attention. Anything else would have risked certain death.

"The prisoners in the House of the Chosen are being prepared to make the ultimate sacrifice to our lord, The Inca," Teacher

Condor noted with emphasis. Then he began to relate the customs of the Incas at the passing of one ruler and the installation of another. Children of conquered tribes were carefully chosen and brought to live in thatched-roof houses where they would be fed and cared for in anticipation of their participation in the holy rite of passage.

A chosen few would be taken to the priestly altar and sacrificed as precious gifts to the divine. To date, the students had witnessed only animal sacrifice to appease the gods, but with The Inca's death, the gods required greater sacrifice.

The priest leaned forward and lowered his voice to a whisper. "The death of The Inca calls for the sacrifice of human life."

The beating of drums stirred Falcon out of a deep sleep. Dawn had not yet come. The drumming could mean only one thing—The Inca had passed from this world into the next. The drums also heralded the beginning of a three-day fast, the priest had told them. No fires would be lit, and there would be no preparation of meals for the next few days. Everyone would mourn for the beloved Inca.

On the morning of the third day, the entire city throbbed with anticipation. As dawn broke, the royalty and the peasantry made their way to the great square in the city center. All were dressed in their finest woven tunics, and the lords and minor princes wore costly ornaments and jewels with the pride befitting a member of the royal court. With great fanfare servants and attendants carried canopies of gaudy weavings and richly tinted tapestries across the square in magnificent pageantry.

Falcon and Puma quickly put on their finest multicolored robes and wove brilliantly hued parrot feathers into their hair. Today they would also wear the golden bracelets that identified them as members of the priestly caste.

As the first tentative rays of sunshine spread out across the square and struck the lofty turrets, the multitude gave a shout of triumph. The royal musicians filled the air with the sound of flutes and drums, swelling louder and louder as the sun rose high above the towering mountains.

The priests then moved to the altar and held up a huge gold goblet in which the sacred *chicha* was offered to the gods. The fermented corn liquor was offered to the new Inca, who held it high before the gathered multitude before drinking deeply. Then royal court members drank from it in the same manner.

As the musicians struck up the familiar chords of celebration, The Inca and his court led the procession to Sacsayhuaman where the new ruler would be formally crowned.

Puma and Falcon fell in step with the other students from the House of Learning, taking their places behind Teacher Condor. Their teacher followed the royal priests and mentors charged with guarding and upholding Inca religious traditions.

"Look at all those ornaments," Falcon whispered to Puma. The boys could see their fathers just ahead among the royal priests; each wore identical gold robes with flowing, multicolored headdresses. The Inca was carried among them in a royal dais, his commanding presence brooding over the assembled peasantry like the strange power of a gathering storm. Beside the royal dais, attendants carried the richly dressed body of the old Inca.

As the procession wound up the path to the holiest of places— Sacsayhuaman—the vibrant chanting of the priests filled the air with an otherworldly sound. The llamas and alpacas spat in protest as they were herded along behind the pupils from the House of Learning. And following the beasts, the reluctant white-robed members of the House of the Chosen trudged silently.

It took most of the morning for the procession to reach the mighty fortress. Sentries held strict formation as the old and new rulers silently passed through the gates and into the sacred place.

Falcon and Puma gazed in awe as the priests gathered in a tight circle around the new Inca and the body of the former ruler. The gold priestly robes glinted and sparkled in the midday sun as though glowing with an unseen source of light from within. The boys could see that in the center of the circle was a stone table on a stand.

A number of priests moved toward the children from the House of the Chosen and began to lift their voices in a chorus of prayer. As the priests chanted, the wide-eyed children were given goblets of *chicha*, which they sipped tentatively. Then the priests cued the musicians with a wave of their hands, and the drummers and flutists exploded into the chords and rhythms of the ceremony's climax. The priests began to chant to the drumming:

> *"To you, Oh Pachacamac,*
>   *we sacrifice to you.*
> *Let us find your favor.*
>   *As our old emperor passes into your presence,*
> *bless us with this new ruler,*
>   *for you are the creator and ruler of everything . . ."*

As the chanting droned on, a child was laid across the sacred altar, and with one swift movement the priest slit the small throat and then plunged a knife into the heart. The Sun God was appeased. "Blessings on The Inca," the priests chanted, for they had honored his passing with the ultimate sacrifice.

The audience of lords and princes and priests and students and attendants cheered loudly. The new Inca now stood before them and was crowned in the final act of the ancient tradition.

Falcon and Puma stood in stunned silence, staring out across the courtyard. Though Teacher Condor had prepared them for the ceremony, they could not conceal their shock. One day they, too, would conduct the business of the gods, for this was their heritage. But they were glad it would not begin today.

Author's note: While the events in this chapter are fictional, they are based on careful research of the ancient Incas. The rest of this book is about the life of the Quicaña family and of one member in particular—Rómulo Sauñe. Some members of the family believe the Quicañas are the descendants of the Inca royal priesthood. Like the Levites of the Bible, these men and women were a special caste of the Quechua culture charged with maintaining and perpetuating the spiritual life of their people. What you're about to read happened in the highlands of Peru. Through the gospel of Jesus Christ, a people have been transformed. Part of that transformation began in the remote village of Chakiqpampa where a young shepherd boy tended sheep and learned to love the true Creator of all things.

1

The Journey Home

The terminal's public address system blared out the announcement to travelers waiting expectantly for their flights: "This is the final boarding call for Flight 1832 from Quito to Lima."

Rómulo Sauñe smiled and began gathering up his bags. Soon he would wrap his arms around his loved ones in the village high in the Andes of Peru. His friend, a tall, blue-eyed American, settled into the seat next to him on the plane.

As they waited for take-off, Rómulo was filled with joy. "Oh, Heavenly Father," he whispered, "your plans are always so much bigger than ours." They were returning from a groundbreaking conference of Quechua Christians who represented millions of Quechua people throughout Ecuador, Peru, and Bolivia. How grateful he was that the Quechua leaders had also seen the need to join with other Christians—not just Quechuas—who lived throughout the Americas. If they spoke with one voice, perhaps they would be heard and their needs better understood. That was his dream, and now it was beginning to take form.

As the airplane raced down the runway and soared into the sky, Rómulo turned to Al Shannon and smiled widely. "Soon we'll be home!"

Al smiled back, but a hint of worry crossed his face. "What's the matter?" Rómulo asked.

"Rómulo, are you still planning on going up to Ayacucho when we get back to Peru? You know this is one of the worst times with all the activity from the Shining Path."

"Al, my people have suffered so much during these last few years. The least I can do is go and encourage them. You know that almost three years ago my grandfather was killed by the Shining Path in my home village. I never went to the funeral, nor have I paid my respects at his grave. I need to be there with my people on this important anniversary. I just can't stay away from my village any longer."

Al listened respectfully. How he had grown to love the spirit of the Quechua people since he had come as a young missionary with Wycliffe Bible Translators to make his home among them so long ago. No matter the danger, a Quechua was obligated to think of the group first and then of himself.

"You know," Rómulo's voice burst into his thoughts, "during the last few months I've seen a wonderful change in Rumi, my eldest son. He recently turned twelve, and he's beginning to gain a renewed interest in his Quechua heritage. I'm so pleased."

"Rómulo, that's wonderful. What do you think made the difference?"

"I think it must have been the hours of storytelling," Rómulo said with a grin. "Last summer when I drove with Donna and the children across the United States, I would gather the family around me and tell stories from my childhood. I began to teach Rumi about my people and our language. I wanted him to know how much I love my heritage.

"Al," Rómulo added, "I know it will be dangerous up in the mountains. But that's a risk I feel I must take. My family and I have talked a lot about the danger from the Shining Path, and we never talk in terms of *what if* I'm taken. It's a case of *when*.

"You know that my life is in God's hands, Al. If God had wanted to, He could have taken me in an automobile accident in the States where I drove so much. But He didn't. If God should call me home soon, I want to be with my people."

And with that, Rómulo settled back into his seat and gazed out the window. How he hated what the senseless war between the Maoist revolutionary group and the government had done to the land he loved and to his people. The Shining Path had ravaged the city of Ayacucho, the surrounding villages, and a great part of the country for nearly a decade. Killing was indiscriminate and more often than not merely a tactic for instilling terror in the hearts of those who would not join them. But in the effort to bring down the revolutionaries, the army had also spread its terror, and thousands had been caught in the cross-fire. Perhaps no one was more aware of the people who had died than Rómulo. Among them were his people, members of his family, loved ones, and acquaintances.

What had it been like before the Shining Path? His mind drifted back to the wind-whipped canyons and mountainsides of his childhood. There were the sheep he had shepherded from his earliest memories; there was the creek where he had drawn water for his mother; there was the rock where he would sit for hours and play his flute while the animals grazed.

The small boy scrambled over and around the rocks and boulders that dotted the field. He had brought his flock here to graze early in the morning. At four years of age he was proud to have such an important responsibility, but sometimes he was lonely.

Finally he shimmied up a high, flat rock with his bare feet and found a little ledge to lean up against. From here he could clearly see the sheep and goats in the distance as he surveyed the rugged terrain. He didn't mind his tattered shirt and patched pants, but sometimes he longed for a pair of sandals to wear. But no matter. Today was beautiful. He would play his *quena*, or flute, and watch his flock.

Hours later a cold wind gathered strength and whipped up the mountainside. Little Rómulo pulled the collar of his worn shirt closer around his neck and pushed his jet-black hair out of his eyes. The weather was shifting quickly, as it often would, and he thought about gathering up his flock. His empty stomach told him it was nearly time to go home anyway, so perhaps grandfather wouldn't mind if he came in a bit early.

He hopped off the rock and scampered after his flock. The wind buffeted the scrub brush, and the late afternoon sun painted long shadows across the path. Rómulo coaxed the sheep and the goats toward home, nudging the little ones with his staff and yelling at the older ones that stopped to get a last mouthful of grass. Soon both sheep and shepherd would be settled in for the night.

Rómulo's days would begin long before the sun peeked across the mountains behind the family home. "*Hatari, hatari!* Rómulo, get up!" his mother, Zoila, would call. "It's time to pray, little one." Each day the same words roused the family, and soon all the children would gather around her to pray to their Heavenly Father. Since Zoila had come to know the Lord, her life was devoted to prayer. And until everyone came to know her Lord, there would be no rest. So they prayed for each of their relatives by name—that God would touch their hearts and they would all be one in Him.

After prayer Rómulo would walk a mile down the deep ravine to a rushing stream where he would fill two earthen jars with water. His grandmother and his mother used the water to cook their meals. It was an important chore, he knew. He would back out of the ravine and race home, trying not to spill too much of the precious water.

When he reached the family home, he would carefully pour the water into a larger vessel just outside the entryway. The ground around the village of Chakiqpampa was dry as dust because the rains came so seldom. The name meant "place that dries out" or "the arid place," referring to a lagoon that filled up in the rainy season, but then slowly dried out in the dry season, leaving a vast open space.

After a light breakfast of potato soup, Rómulo would head out the door with a staff he had made himself and call the family's flock of sheep and goats. It was only necessary to tie the leader up to a stake. The others would go nowhere without him. And so as dawn broke, Rómulo untied the ram, and together they all set off toward the rolling hills where he would pasture the flock until the sun began to set across the canyons.

One afternoon as he played his *quena* and listened for the echoes to return in haunting repetition, there was a sudden cloudburst in the distance. Rain clouds began to gather speed as they rolled through the valleys, engulfing the mountain peaks and high meadows in a mantle of fog.

Startled, Rómulo reached for his staff and raced to gather his flock before they spooked and ran every which way. As he called out to them, he caught sight of a lone figure running toward him in the mist. Rómulo could make out the flowing gray beard—a sign of distinction worn solely by the patriarch of Rómulo's clan—and the warm smile of his maternal grandfather, Justiniano Quicaña. The family respectfully and lovingly called him Abraham, for he was more than just the grandfather. He was the bearer of the family history and the legends of the Incas.

"Grandfather!" Rómulo hollered. "Why are you here?"

"I saw the rain and came to find you, little Rómulo. Where is Arca? Wasn't he near you?" Grandfather scanned the horizon for his son Arcangel. Uncle Arcangel and nephew Rómulo were less than a year apart and inseparable friends. Grandfather knew that they often grazed their flocks together to keep each other company.

"Arcangel was here, Grandfather, but later he moved his flock farther down the mountainside. He's probably on his way home by now."

"You keep moving toward the village, Rómulo," Grandfather instructed. "I'll see if I can catch up with him."

He waved good-bye and disappeared into the gathering storm. Soon Rómulo was running down the last trail home, anxiously waving his staff over the bleating flock, afraid that the crack of thunder and lightning would send the sheep scurrying in all directions. Moments later the flock had safely gathered round the house.

The Quicaña home was one of about eighty in the village. Outside the house lay a huge rock with intricate carvings on all sides. Just about anyone who happened to come by for a visit was offered a chance to lift it and test his strength. One day Rómulo asked his grandfather about the unusual rock.

"Oh, this large rock has been around for centuries, Rómulo," the old man replied with a knowing smile. "It's one of the original rocks your ancestors brought here from the quarries nearby. I found it in some ancient ruins and carted it to the house years ago. It's a work of art." As he talked, the old man ran his hands along the smooth surface, his fingers tracing the intricate patterns carved into the sides.

Had Rómulo been a stranger to this house, he would have likely jumped in fright when he pushed open the door to the largest room. The *depósito*, or storage room, was filled with shadows and strange shapes. But Rómulo was not afraid of this room because here were grandfather's treasures. Over the years Grandfather Quicaña, a born treasure hunter, had collected amazing and unusual artifacts which he lovingly restored and used to decorate his home—old pots, bits of gold, jewelry, carved stones, and even ancient mummies.

In one dark corner of the storeroom, a figure appeared to be leaning against the wall. But as one's eyes became accustomed to the dark, the figure took on the shape of a mummy. Its translucent skin, its yellowing, silky tufts of hair attached to a pock-marked skull, its arms wrapped around a fleshless set of bony legs tucked up against the leatherlike chest were a ghastly sight to a stranger. But to the family, it was just another object. The mummies were the most unusual objects in Justiniano's infamous "museum," as the locals referred to it. When threads of light worked their way down through the rafters, the mummies glowed with a yellowish light of their own.

"Grandfather, why do we have these mummies of our ancestors in the *depósito?* None of the other children have such things in their houses," Rómulo asked one day.

Justiniano was pleased at Rómulo's interest. After thinking for a few moments, the old sage stroked his beard and said, "Rómulo, that's a good question." As though looking into the past, Justiniano's eyes gazed out beyond Rómulo, coming to rest on the surrounding hills that hid great mysteries still to be revealed.

"Do you remember that I once told you that the Quicañas were of the caste of the royal priests of The Inca?" he began. "The mummies you see here are from that wonderful period in our history. Caring for our ancestors was an important part of the rituals. The priests ensured that the passage from this life to the next be properly attended to.

"There is a legend that tells of a young girl who was disrespectful toward one of the sacred mummies. Her bones disintegrated, and she died a terrible death. We don't want that curse to fall on us, little one, and that is why we treat all that is from our past with great respect and care. It was our caste's responsibility to usher the great Inca leaders into the next world with all they would need to survive as the royals that they were here in this life."

"But that was way back then. Why do we have them now? Why are they in our house?" Rómulo persisted as he pointed to the mummy leaning up against the wall. "Why do you keep all these old things in the *depósito?*"

"Oh, little Rómulo, through the years I've discovered all these old relics in the fields and in caves, and I've brought them here because they are our link with the past. Someone must remember and pass this on to other generations. None of it can be lost, do you understand? It is the Inca way, it's the Quicaña way, and it must be your way," he replied with a kindly tone in his usually gruff voice.

2
Land of Gold Treasure

Soon after Rómulo was born, his father, Enrique, left the family. Drifting from village to village, he took odd jobs here and there, but never came home long enough to take any interest in the family business. Rómulo's mother had to return to her parents' household and live under their authority and guidance, as did all of her children.

In the Quicaña household, Rómulo and Arca competed for Grandfather's attention. Sometimes they even ate off of each other's plates. But more than anything, they deeply loved each other.

One afternoon as the two young shepherds urged their flocks toward home, other children from Chakiqpampa ran out to meet them.

"Come on, Rómulo, I'll race you home," Arcangel shouted across the meadow. Eight-year-old Rómulo herded the flock across the tundra as fast as he could, but Arcangel was better at this and beat him home before he had even really got started.

As they finished tying up the lead ram, Rómulo turned to his playmates and suggested, "Let's race on the pigs!"

The other children squealed with joy and eagerly ran after him as he chased down an old sow. Arcangel had already grabbed his pig for the race, and several other boys had theirs in tow.

Huffing and puffing, Rómulo threw his arms around the pig and brought it to an abrupt halt. The others lined up their pigs next to his. With a triumphant shout, Rómulo yelled, "Go!" They all hopped on, and the pigs took off like a shot, racing every which way but straight ahead. Rómulo screamed with laughter as the pig screeched and tried to buck him off.

"Rómulo is winning! Rómulo is winning!" shouted one little boy. Everyone wanted Rómulo to win—but not before they all had had a good ride. As one boy tumbled off, another regained his balance, and still Rómulo rode his crazed mount.

Suddenly, Rómulo's pig took a sharp turn and headed straight toward a pack of horses. Rómulo tightened his grip around the pig's neck and tried to guide it away from the dangerous hooves. Horses didn't like anything underfoot, and no one knew that better than Rómulo. He sensed the danger, but he couldn't bring himself to roll off the pig. That would be defeat. But just as the pig brushed past, one of the horses nervously bucked and kicked out at the pig. Instead of kicking the pig, the rear legs of the horse found their mark with a loud whack on Rómulo's head.

The boy tumbled off in a daze and lay slumped on the ground. The world was spinning, and then it turned black.

"Rómulo! Rómulo!" shouted one of his brothers as he tried to move him. But the sight of blood trickling out of Rómulo's ears sent him running off to the woodshed to hide in terror. The squeals and the laughter stopped suddenly, and all the children ran out to the field where Rómulo lay still and seemingly lifeless. An older boy ran back to the Quicaña house for help.

Grandfather Justiniano came running out and knelt by Rómulo. He checked to see if Rómulo was breathing. He was— barely. Then he lifted him up and carried him back to the house with a trail of frightened children behind.

He lay Rómulo down on a pallet. While Zoila wiped away the

blood, Grandfather Justiniano mixed a medicinal paste of herbs which he spread over the wound on Rómulo's temple.

With a shiver Rómulo opened his eyes and tried to talk. "What happened?"

"Shh," Grandfather calmed him. "Don't talk. You've had quite a blow to your head."

Rómulo's ears were ringing, and his head felt sluggish and heavy. "What, Grandfather? I can't hear you . . . Did I win the race?"

"No one won. You got hurt."

"Ohhhhh. My head is pounding," he cried. Tears streamed down his cheeks. Grandfather tenderly wiped them away. The village was so isolated that there was little chance of getting him to a doctor. The nearest village was too far to walk with an injured child. It would be better to pray and to apply the ancient medicine of the Andes. As far as the villagers were concerned, Justiniano was the closest thing to a doctor anyway, for he knew the secrets of the herbs and the plants and all living things that grew in their part of the world.

In the days that followed, Rómulo gradually recovered, but the ache in his head and the ringing in his ears was incessant. Weeks later the pounding and the ringing stopped, and the raw wound on his temple healed leaving no permanent scar. Soon he was back on his feet playing with the other children and pasturing his flock. But some things had changed. The hearing in one of his ears was gone, and he had difficulty understanding instruction. The village children cruelly bestowed a new name on Rómulo— *Opa,* or Deaf and Stupid One.

SLAM. Grandfather and Rómulo quickly entered the house to escape the cold wind that blew off the distant snow-capped peaks. Rómulo slipped over to Arca who sat in a corner looking at a small Spanish language book. "Read me something, Arca."

"Want to read it yourself?" Arca kidded him. Since the accident Rómulo had developed learning disabilities. No matter how hard he tried, he could not absorb any instruction at school. The hearing loss made it even more difficult. But still he kept trying.

"Why, you little dog!" Rómulo yelled as he jumped on Arca and wrestled him to the floor. "You know I can't read yet."

Arcangel squirmed out from under Rómulo and with a quick move pinned him to the floor. "When are you going to learn to read, Rómulo? It's time, isn't it?"

Rómulo struggled to get out from under his uncle, but it was no use. Arca was bigger. Rómulo's body went limp. "I give up, you win. Now let me up."

Arca rolled off and sat on the floor laughing. "Okay, Rómulo. I'll read you something." Arca slowly read a few pages of his Spanish reader. Spanish was a new language to them, and they struggled to get through the words. Rómulo was determined to learn to read so he tried to follow along. Why couldn't they learn to read in Quechua? What was wrong with their own language, he wondered.

When Rómulo was eight years old, he began attending school in the nearby village of Anta. It was about three miles from Chakiqpampa and a long walk for a boy. But for Rómulo, it was nothing. Each day the round-trip trek for water was nearly that long. So his legs were used to it, and he and Arca played as they ran down the trail.

His first grade teacher ruled the class with a large stick. For a mistake or an error, he would whack the student on the head. It was humiliating. The teacher didn't understand Quechua, and many of the students didn't understand Spanish. So the whacks were frequent, intended to keep order as much as to teach a lesson.

After a time some of the students got tired of being whacked and struggling with the new language, and they just dropped out. There was plenty to do in the village and in the outlying communities where many of the students lived, so no one paid much attention to the importance of an education.

But despite the difficulties, Rómulo refused to give up. Even as Arca moved on to second and third grade, leaving Rómulo hopelessly mired in first, Rómulo still kept going to class hoping one day it would all make sense to him. The second time around, he took the tests and passed with an average of 12, the lowest passing grade on a scale of 1 to 20. But when Rómulo eagerly listened for his name on the list of second graders, it wasn't read out.

"You can't come into second grade, Rómulo," the teacher told him as he quietly walked past his desk at the end of the day. "You have to pass with a better grade. A 12 isn't enough. I'm sorry."

Rómulo nodded. He was doomed to repeat first grade, but he determined that one day he would pass.

After two years at the same school, Arcangel and Rómulo switched to the Paccha school—seven miles from Chakiqpampa. Arca would be in the third grade, and Rómulo would try again with first grade. For all the walking on the rough footpaths to Paccha, Rómulo finally received his first pair of sandals. Each morning Grandmother would wrap a simple lunch of a cooked potato for each of them, which they would tuck into their pockets and eat with the other students during recess.

One day Uncle Fernando, Arcangel's older brother, approached the boys and asked if they would stop by the bakery in Paccha on their way home from school. He gave them ten *soles* to buy enough bread for the entire household. The boys stared wide-eyed at the money—it was enough to hire a man to work half a day in the field!

"Now, I know it will be hard for you boys to walk all the way home without eating some of the bread," Fernando said, "so you can go ahead and eat one *sol's* worth of bread. But bring the rest home for the family."

As they reached the town early that morning, Rómulo suggested, "Let's buy a *sol's* worth of bread right now. I can't wait until after school."

"Great idea," Arcangel said. "Better yet. Let's buy eight *soles'* worth."

From the bakery to the school, the two munched on the bread. The rest they stored inside their school desk along with the remaining two *soles*. When they came in from midmorning recess, they checked their hidden treasure. Most of it was gone! Someone had eaten some of the family bread and stolen all the money. There were only three rolls of bread left.

The boys began to cry. "Now what are we going to tell Fernando?" Arcangel asked. "He'll never trust us again now that we've lost his ten *soles*."

The boys hung onto the three rolls through the remainder of the day and cast suspicious looks at their fellow students. At the end of the day, the teacher suggested that everyone go together down to the local swimming hole. Arcangel and Rómulo hung back. It was difficult to get excited about a swim when a spanking was waiting back home.

When the class reached the stream, the boys suddenly cheered up at the prospect of a cool swim. They placed the remaining bread in a cloth and left it on top of a flat rock. Then they raced to the swimming hole and dove in with the other boys. A few minutes later, they glanced back up to the rock on shore, and to their surprise a donkey had ambled by and was eating their bread—cloth and all!

"Hey, you mule!" Arcangel shouted. Rómulo began to cry again.

"Well," Arcangel said philosophically after the bread was entirely gone and the donkey had moved on to a more interesting section of the beach, "we might as well have fun since we're already here."

Rómulo wiped away his tears, but the fear of going home empty-handed gnawed at him. Finally the teacher sent all the boys home, and Arcangel and Rómulo began the long trudge back to Chakiqpampa. But as the sun dipped behind the mountain range to the west and the trail grew darker, they became disoriented.

As they forded a fast-moving brook, Rómulo's foot got stuck between two rocks, and his sandal floated downstream. "My sandal!" Rómulo screamed. Arcangel jumped back into the brook, and together they chased down the floating sandal.

Darkness was setting in, and the boys began to fear they would never find their way home. Arcangel led the way down another trail that took them across another stream—this one much deeper than the first. As they crossed over a narrow log bridge, Rómulo slipped and fell headfirst into the icy water.

"Rómulo!" Arcangel yelled out. "Hold on to the rocks!" But his voice was drowned out as Rómulo was carried downstream.

Finally Rómulo managed to grab onto a rock. When Arcangel waded in to get him, Rómulo gasped, "I've lost both my sandals!"

Arcangel tried to see where they might have gone, but it was too dark. The sandals were lost forever.

Late in the evening, the boys trudged into Grandfather Justiniano's house. Grandmother Teofila was resting by the fire, waiting for the boys to come home. The other children were already put to bed, and only she and Zoila remained awake. The boys stood in the middle of the room shivering with cold, tears streaming down their faces.

"Boys, what happened? You're so late!" Teofila exclaimed as she hugged her son, Arcangel, and Zoila knelt down by Rómulo. "Why are you crying?" Grandmother Teofila asked in a gentle voice.

When they had told her the whole sad story, Teofila leaned back. "Well, that's an awful story. But don't worry. We won't say anything to Grandfather and Fernando. They went away preaching, so they needn't know what's happened. I'll pay for the bread, and it will be our secret."

The next day the bread was fresh from the bakery when Fernando and Justiniano came marching in from their preaching trip.

Several months later, when the family had settled down for the night, Rómulo lay in bed watching the fire slowly die out. Then a thought crossed his mind. "Grandfather," he called out. The old man was sitting across the room examining an artifact he had found that day in his potato field. "Grandfather," Rómulo called out again, "did you find that today?"

"Yes, Rómulo, I found this gold nugget as I walked through a field early this morning. I saw a glint in the ground and dug around it with my knife. Here it is."

Justiniano carried the nugget over to his inquisitive grandson. He let him turn it over in his small hand and feel its smooth surface.

"But it's not the real treasure—the great gold," Justiniano said as he tossed the nugget into an aluminum cooking pot. "That's the Quechua or great gold. I'll find it someday."

"Grandfather, isn't there a family legend about when our Inca ancestors hid the gold from the Spaniards? I can't remember it. Could you tell it again?"

Grandfather made himself comfortable and settled into the story. "Oh, Rómulo, you have so many questions. Well, here's what I know about the gold. When the Spanish conquerors began to invade our world, they wanted the treasure of the Incas. They weren't interested in our science or our knowledge of the stars, nor did they care about the medicines in the earth. All they wanted was the gold and the precious stones.

"So our ancestors hid what little gold remained in *tapadas*. And they buried them in the ground. Sometimes they also hid them in the caves or wherever they thought the Spanish wouldn't find them. Over time gases seemed to build up inside the *tapadas* which could kill a treasure hunter if he breathed them in. Everybody knows this. That's why I've told you ever since you were small to stay away from the *tapadas* if you find them. But I know the secret of opening them without harm. Today, if you go looking for the gold, and a snake crosses your path, you will be sure to find it. At least that is what the legend claims.

"Once my grandfather was working in his fields. At about midday his daughter, the woman who became my mother, took his lunch to him. As she walked across the field toward him, my grandfather's foot-plow pushed into one of these *tapadas*. It was filled with jewels.

"Well, he was so startled by the discovery of the rich treasure that he didn't know what to do except to quickly rebury it. He didn't want anyone else to find it. His daughter was so afraid of the power of the treasure that she told the people in the surrounding communities to stay away from that field. Such was the fear that no one came near the place, and to this day no one even remembers where the *tapada* was.

"But my mother did keep one thing from the *tapada*. Do you know what that was, Rómulo?"

"No, Grandfather," he said, his voice laced with anticipation. "What was it?"

"She kept the flat stone cover of the *tapada* and brought it home. We still have it. You know what it is—that smooth rock we use to grind our grain."

"But, Grandfather, did anyone ever find that *tapada* again? Have you tried to find it?"

"Most of my life, Rómulo," the bearded man replied with a sigh. "But I've never found it."

Night after night, when the fire would die down and everyone would drift off to bed, Rómulo often sat by his grandfather listening to the tales from the past. Grandfather hoped that Rómulo would be the person who would carry the family history to the next generation. Justiniano loved many things in his grandson, but most of all he was pleased that they shared the same love for their past and for the future.

And sometimes Justiniano would tell Rómulo about how God had helped him in recent years. It was all meant to teach Rómulo about life and the importance of faith. The old man was confident that God would lead their family in the years ahead. He could already sense the vision filling Rómulo's young heart. The wonders God had prepared for this wide-eyed boy caused his heart to overflow with gratitude. Somehow God would find a way to help this boy learn the lessons he would need to learn as he began his walk through life. But old Justiniano could never have imagined the great distance God would take this handicapped boy and the remarkable task God had for him.

If there was one thing Justiniano regretted, it was that none of his children or other grandchildren shared Rómulo's excitement for the stories from the past. Regardless of his listeners' lack of enthusiasm, Grandfather often launched into his tales over dinner when the family would gather after a long day's work in the fields. The Inca treasure, he would remind them, is still buried out there in the mountains. There was a mine that had so much of the lost treasure that it flowed like a waterfall and pooled into a vast lake of pure gold. The place was called by the Quechua name, "Grandson of the Great Gold," or *Qorehuilca*.

Many years later when Rómulo was in his midtwenties, the young man showed up at the family home in Chakiqpampa with a metal detector.

"Now, grandfather," he announced with great fanfare, "we can search for the lost treasure of the Incas!"

Grandfather laughed with joy. "Oh my, you're serious about this, aren't you?"

Rómulo proudly demonstrated how the detector worked. "Grandfather, let's go find that lost gold mine you always used to tell us about!"

Rómulo's enthusiasm sparked something in the old man. After all these years of dreaming about Inca gold, the thought of mounting an expedition to find it was almost more than he could stand. With great excitement, he brought the family together and announced, "It's time to look for the Inca treasure."

Everyone in the family began talking at once. But the only one who really believed the treasure was out there was Rómulo. Fernando muttered, "Father, it's just a dream. It's just a legend. I don't think there's any gold."

Rómulo's brother Ruben chimed in, "No one has ever found the gold. No one ever will."

The house was full of skeptics, but Rómulo stood beside his grandfather and declared, "Why are you so certain there's no gold? Grandfather is going to show us the way."

The next day they began to plan the expedition. Everyone in Chakiqpampa was excited. Justiniano agreed to take anyone who wanted to go, and he proudly told the villagers about the metal detector. His enthusiasm infected the whole community.

Several days later, the Quicaña clan and several other villagers started on their great adventure. As they traveled down the mountain trail, Rómulo asked, "Do you remember exactly where the gold mine is located, Grandfather?"

"Oh, yes, I remember very clearly where I once saw that gold. I've seen it in all its splendor."

As Arcangel, Rómulo, and his brothers picked their way along the mountain footpaths, Justiniano entertained them with tales of their ancient Inca ancestors. Proudly they rode their horses all day, each taking a turn carrying the metal detector as though it were a great prize. Occasionally they would stop to rest in a wooded glen and feast on the treats Grandmother Teofila had prepared for the special occasion.

After traveling for many hours, Justiniano suddenly reined in his horse and shaded his eyes to gaze across a small valley. He pointed to a foothill in the mountains surrounding them.

"That's it," he proclaimed. "There's the gold."

The boys spurred their horses on and raced across the meadow. Unloading their gear, they waited for Grandfather to catch up. Then Rómulo stepped forward. "Where should we look, Grandfather?"

Grandfather just stood there thinking silently. The others were growing impatient.

Arcangel paced back and forth. "Here, Father, or here? Where should we dig?"

Still Grandfather appeared lost in thought. In the meantime, the expedition had attracted a few curious members of the surrounding hamlets. "What are you doing?" they asked.

Rómulo proudly explained, "This is my grandfather—a direct descendant of Inca royalty. He is going to show us where the Inca gold is."

"Oh," they said. "Can we help?"

"Sure," said Rómulo. He loved a crowd. But Arcangel frowned at him.

Still Grandfather remained silent. The locals prompted him, "We should look over there." They pointed toward a mound near the entrance of a small cave.

Then Grandfather spoke up. "It's in the cave." Joyously everybody grabbed something to dig with and rushed up the hill to the entrance. Soon they were all digging in the dry soil. To their great excitement, the needle on the detector's gauge swung to the highest point. "The gold must be here," they kept babbling to each other.

The hours spun past, but the dreams of a fortune in gold kept them going, moving about like ants on an anthill. What they didn't know was that the soil was full of metallic ore. Frustration gnawed at them as they dug on, finding no gold.

Finally, as the sun began to set behind the mountains, Rómulo and the others approached Justiniano. One of the locals said respectfully, "Let's wait until tomorrow, and then we will take you to another place where we've seen gold before." Others agreed. Everyone had seen gold somewhere at sometime.

The next day, off they went with the metal detector. But again they found nothing. Finally the Quicañas had run out of food and hope. It was time to go home. They all surrounded Grandfather trying not to look accusing. Grandfather had seemed so confident, so sure of himself; his stories were so full of adventure! Was there any truth to them?

Now they sat quietly on makeshift logs along a rippling stream. No one spoke. Feeling their frustration, Grandfather decided he had to say something. "Gentlemen," he barked out with all the dignity he could muster, "it's been many years since I saw that treasure. Just because we can't find it doesn't mean it isn't there. We may have been inches from finding it or miles from the location I remembered. Let's go back home and perhaps on another day when my memory is clearer, we'll form another expedition and search in the right place. It will be glorious!"

Suddenly the thought of going home empty-handed to Grandmother and everyone else in Chakiqpampa crossed everyone's mind. Someone began to giggle, and finally they all burst into laughter, keeping it up until tears streamed down their faces. The few people who lived in this remote region would say they were a hopeless lot, but who cared? The expedition had been a wonderful time of togetherness and something they would never forget.

Despite his disappointment, Rómulo joined in the laughter. And seeing his grandfather standing there with a grin stretched across his face, the young man offered some encouragement. "Oh, Grandfather, one day you'll remember exactly where the treasure is. And when you do, I'll be the first to take you there. No one will be laughing when we come back loaded down with the gold of our ancestors."

3

The First of Many to Believe

As the plane carrying Rómulo Sauñe and Al Shannon prepared to land in Peru, Rómulo could hardly contain his excitement. His luggage was jammed with gifts for friends and relatives. It was an old Quechua custom that the traveler return with gifts. Soon he would be with his people face to face, and they would talk of the wonderful blessings of the Lord. He would also hear their sorrowful stories firsthand.

He knew that many of his friends and acquaintances had suffered, and their hearts were full of fear and dread. The violence that surrounded them day after day had worn down their spirits; many mourned for those who were maimed; many wept for those who simply disappeared in the night, only to be found in the morning lying dead along the well-trodden trails of the isolated Quechua communities.

When the friends and families would trudge reluctantly down to military headquarters to ask the whereabouts of the young men hauled away in the night, they were crudely rebuffed. "Why do you want to know? Who sent you? Are you collaborators with the terrorists?" the sentry would spit out, as though a mother had no right to know what had happened to her son.

Respect for life had evaporated. It was better to live in fear than to ask the difficult questions. Better not to know that your son was tortured to death. Better not to know why the world is never an easy place for the Quechua.

The voices of his family and friends often echoed in Rómulo's mind. *Do not forsake us. Remember our pain.* And Rómulo never forgot. Tears flowed easily when he talked of his people. *The world must know of our suffering. They cannot ignore the cries of the brethren anymore.*

The modest gifts he carried would bring simple pleasure and encouragement to his people. Just the thought that someone beyond their village remembered them would be the highlight of his visit for many.

As his luggage rolled down the ramp and onto the carousel in the Lima airport, Rómulo noticed a lock from one of his suitcases hanging open. Something was wrong! He had carefully fastened everything as he had checked his bags in the Quito airport. When he lifted the suitcase off the carousel, it was surprisingly light. Quickly, he took it to the side and opened it. To his horror, all the presents had been cleaned out.

Rómulo gathered up his things with a heavy heart. Now he would have to go shopping to find other suitable gifts. What a waste. He maneuvered through the doorway with his bags and suitcases and then spotted Al waiting for him. Al sympathized with him over the missing gifts.

Rómulo wanted to travel home to Chosica, a suburb of Lima about one-hour's drive from the airport. But the 11 P.M. curfew was too close.

"Looks like you're stuck with me for another night," Al said. "Why don't you stay overnight with Barbara and me in our guest room? It'll be no problem. Let me go give her a call."

While Al dialed home, Rómulo's eyes wandered around the terminal. Suddenly he spied an old friend. He rushed over and they embraced. The friend, a taxi driver, offered to take him back to Chosica. "Wonderful!" Rómulo exclaimed.

Al hung up the phone, and Rómulo informed him, "Al, guess what? I've run into a friend who is a taxi driver. He's going to give me a lift home."

The two men shook hands and embraced. Little did Al know that this would be their last good-bye, the last time he would see the dignified, charismatic Rómulo Sauñe—in this life.

As Rómulo and his friend drove off into the darkness, Rómulo rejoiced in the provision of the Lord Jesus. God took care of even the smallest details. *How blessed we are,* he thought. And then his mind wandered back in time.

"Tell me again, Grandfather. Tell me about how our people came to Chakiqpampa," the young Rómulo prompted his grandfather Justiniano Quicaña.

"You want to hear that story again?"

Rómulo nodded. His eyes sparkled with anticipation.

"Well," Justiniano began, "our Quicaña family wore the priestly robes of the Inca nation. In Cuzco they were part of the priestly caste in the *Tawantinsuyu.* Do you know what that word means, little one? It means as far as the Inca territory extended to the four corners of the earth."

Rómulo snuggled up close to his grandfather and listened attentively.

"When the Spaniards conquered our people, the Quicañas moved from Copacabana, a town to the south near Lake Titicaca, and together with three other families they settled in the town of Paccha. These four families put their names on markers outlining the four corners of the town square. The next time you go to Paccha, you should look for the markers. They're still there.

"Rómulo, my grandfather once told me about a temple of gold that was hidden in Paccha. To this day it is still hidden, but I know one day it will be discovered," Grandfather said with a knowing smile.

"My father moved the family here to the village of Chakiqpampa, which is one of three villages that belong to the greater community. But the ownership of the whole area fell into the hands of a Catholic order of nuns. So, as was customary for the Spanish, all the people on the land became indentured servants of the Catholic church."

"But didn't you live away from Chakiqpampa for some time, Grandfather?"

"Yes, Romi, but that's a part of my life I'd just as soon forget. It was before I knew the Lord. I knew only violence to settle differences with my enemies," he said pensively as he stroked his gray beard.

After a slight pause, he conceded, "You might as well know the truth. Before you were born and when your Uncle Fernando was only about four years old, a cattle rustler came into our area. He stole fifty horses from our family. I knew who had taken them, but the authorities wouldn't do anything about it. So I laid a trap and caught the rustler in the act. I took justice into my own hands, and I killed him." Justiniano shook his head at the thought of it.

"The authorities don't understand the value our animals have to us. I knew they would arrest me, so I took our other farm animals to some friends in a nearby community for safekeeping. And one night I took the family, and we fled to a place far from here— to the jungle where it is easy to hide.

"I know it was hard on everyone, but something good did come from it. I learned about God, the Creator, and the Bible for the very first time," Grandfather said.

"What do you mean?"

"Hiding in the jungle for those seven years must seem terrible to someone who doesn't understand. But I was doing what I thought was right. One day as I walked down the street in

Huanta, a missionary came up to me and gave me a Bible. I began to read this book every day. And I found fascinating stories."

Swoosh went the door. Fernando, Rómulo's uncle, strode into the room, took off his hat, and settled into a chair in the kitchen next to the stove. "The fire feels good after a long day," Fernando said as he warmed his hands. Spying his father sitting on a bed with Rómulo curled up next to him, he smiled. "What are you two doing? Talking about the past again?"

Rómulo smiled shyly. Fernando was so big and strong. Why would he care about a little boy? But he did, and he always took time to explain things to him. There was a genuine affection between the two. Fernando reached over and tousled his hair. "What a rascal you are, keeping your grandfather up late again."

Grandfather piped up, "Rómulo asked me to tell about the ancient Incas, and I was just about to tell about the Lord and how we found Him. But I think maybe you should tell the story, Fernando. After all, you came to know Jesus before me! I was just telling Rómulo that Brother Homer gave me a Bible, and that's where I learned the stories I used to tell you when you were a boy."

Fernando smiled, his eyes exuding warmth and joy. "All right, Father, if you insist."

Turning to Rómulo, Fernando began to explain, "When your grandfather got that Bible from the missionary, Homer Emerson, I loved to hear him read the stories about Abraham and Joseph and Moses. Your mother and I would sit by the fire at night and hear these wonderful tales. Later Zoila and I were the first in our family to believe in Jesus Christ."

"My mother was one of the first believers in Chakiqpampa?" Rómulo asked. "Tell me how it happened."

Fernando reached for a Bible sitting on the kitchen table, and he held it in his hands.

"One day when I was in Ayacucho, the biggest city near our village, I ran into two evangelists, and I invited them to visit us in Chakiqpampa. They didn't speak Quechua, but they came anyway, and when they shared the good news about Jesus with us, I translated as much as I could. The verse they taught us was John 3:16, 'For God so loved the world, that He gave His only son that whosoever believed in Him should not perish but have everlasting life.'

"When Zoila heard those words, she was so moved that she immediately put her faith in God. In an instant she understood that God loved her and sent His Son Jesus for her. God's truth just came into her heart, and her life was transformed."

"Yes," Grandfather Justiniano recalled, "and it made me sad that she had become a Christian. After all, we had been taught that evangelicals were of the devil and that they grew long tails and all that rubbish. The Catholic priests always used to tell us to stay away from them. I even used to beat your mother so the devil wouldn't make her grow a tail. That's what we thought we had to do."

Rómulo's eyes opened wide. The thought of people growing tails fascinated him!

"About that time your father left the village, Rómulo, and he began to travel around the country looking for work," Fernando continued. "One day when he came back from one of his trips, your mother told him how the Lord had changed her life. And she tried to tell Enrique about this Jesus who had given His life for her.

"'That may be fine for you, but it's not for me—that's the demon in you talking,' Enrique said. 'You should return to the old ways of our people. The old ways are our ways; we shouldn't be bringing anything foreign into this family. We could be cursed. The spirit of the mountain could bring terrible things upon our family. What you need is to drink some *chicha* to bring you to your senses.'

"But Zoila stood firm. 'I can't turn my back on Christ,

Enrique,' Zoila pleaded. 'He has changed my life. The Almighty God now lives in my heart, and gives me peace and hope.'

"'If that's how it is, then I'm going to leave you and live my own life, Zoila. You can have the children and stay here in your father's house. I don't care.' Enrique stormed out of the house.

"Zoila was sad for a long time. But she told Enrique that if he wanted to leave her, that was for him to decide, but she wouldn't abandon her Lord.

"Enrique packed his belongings and left. No one saw him for several years. But Zoila never stopped praying for him, and she remained faithful to him," Fernando recounted.

"For years I had bad thoughts about Christians," Grandfather picked up the story. "Years ago when my mother died, she asked us not to mourn her death in the usual way with black ribbons and drinking. You know how the wakes are, Romi. I was such a drunk that before she died, she told my sister not to allow me to bury her.

"At first I honored my mother's request. But then I began to have second thoughts. My mother might end up in Hell if we didn't properly mourn her death. I thought that our mourning would refresh her. That's why we mourn our dead. I wanted to hold a mass to pray for her soul, but just in case that was just another tale taught to us by the priests to get our money, I made a trip to Huanta to talk to the foreign missionaries about it."

Smiling at the memory, Grandfather recalled, "You see, Romi, our people have always been afraid of the spirits of the mountains. We knew a bit about the Virgin Mary, about Christianity, but we didn't know much more than that.

"Now this was long ago and I said, 'Teofila, if I talk with a priest, surely he will tell me to hold a mass for my mother. That's what they tell us is the right thing to do. But I know it's to get more money for their churches. Instead, I think we should ask the missionaries what we should do. If they tell me to do a mass, then I'll know it's right.'

"When we reached Huanta, we asked around for the missionaries. The people would tell us, 'Those devils live over there.' Then they would ask us, 'Why are you looking for those devils?'

"I didn't care what they said. Finally we reached the house where the foreigners lived. When the woman opened the door, she didn't understand anything we said. And we couldn't understand her. After a few minutes of this, your grandmother and I just walked away. *Two days of travel wasted,* we thought.

"But back to how the gospel came to us. Fernando was also one of the first in our entire community to believe in Jesus."

"I remember wanting to become an evangelical, and you wanted me to be a priest," Fernando said.

"Yes, that would have been the proper thing to do," Grandfather said. "But one day all that changed when one of those poor souls who trades goat skins from village to village came to Chakiqpampa. I couldn't understand how a goat-skin seller could know about the things of God."

Fernando jumped into the story, "The man was a Christian, and I wanted to learn more about it, but it was hard to understand him because he didn't speak Quechua. But I knew he was of the Lord because I could sense God's love flowing in his life. Patiently he talked to me about John 3 and the man who came to Jesus in the night."

Tears welled up in Fernando's eyes at the joyful memory. "Despite the trouble communicating, I finally said, 'Brother, I want to give myself to the Lord.' Then I knelt down right in the middle of the road where we had been walking, and I gave my life to Jesus Christ."

"When you came back, you looked different," Justiniano chimed in.

"I was full of joy at what Jesus had done in my life, but I didn't know how to explain it to anyone. Romi, my father called me over and asked, 'Fernando, what has happened to you? Are you drunk?'

"It was hard for me to see that my family didn't understand the gospel or what it meant to give yourself to the Lord. I told everyone in the family, and they listened patiently while I tried to preach to them. I felt like Moses when he first went to the Israelites. Somehow I knew, though, that the gospel would one day shine brightly in our little village. But at that time my father, your grandfather, Rómulo, ignored my talks about Jesus Christ and continued drinking more than ever."

"How exciting," Rómulo said as he curled up even closer to Grandfather. "But when did you believe in Jesus Christ, Grandfather?"

"I was fifty years old, little one. It happened a few months later. In my heart I knew that I needed to know this Jesus, but I didn't want to get the gospel from some old goat-skin trader. It seemed undignified to me. I wanted to hear the gospel from somebody official—like a pastor. So one day Fernando and I walked down to Huamanga. That's the city also known as Ayacucho."

"But you weren't in very good shape when we got to the pastor's house, were you, Father?" Fernando said with a slight grin.

"No," Justiniano confessed. "We made the mistake of stopping by my Uncle Oswaldo Matilla's house first, and he offered me a drink. I said, 'Okay, just one last time.' Fernando stood there watching me, and I could see he was disgusted with me as I proceeded to get stone drunk. He kept trying to pull me away, but soon Uncle Oswaldo and I had guzzled an entire bottle of liquor.

"Finally Fernando dragged me away, and we stumbled down the street to Pastor Simon Izarra's house. I was completely drunk. Fernando knocked on the door and asked to see the pastor. When this young man came to the door, he could see I was in no condition to talk. He told us to go away and come back when I was sober."

"But we had walked such a long way," Fernando picked up

the story, "that I didn't want to go back without my father having received the Lord. I explained this to the pastor, and he reluctantly invited us in."

Justiniano added, "I had so many questions about who this God was and how He was different from the gods we had worshiped for centuries—the sun and the spirits. This pastor told me about Jesus Christ and patiently answered all my questions." Grandfather paused to chuckle. "I must have been revolting as I sat there drunk, chewing on a large ball of coca leaves.

"As I sat there slumped over in the chair, Brother Izarra said, 'Why don't you come back tomorrow morning to receive Christ? You'll be in better shape.' But I was insistent. I hadn't come all that way to wait until the morning to receive Christ. 'Are you irresponsible?' I bellowed out. 'Make me receive right now!' I ordered him to pray with me. And then I fell to my knees, and with tears streaming down my face I gave my life to the Lord. The pastor was so surprised he fell to his knees too, and he prayed for me. When I stood up, I was a changed man. It was the last time I ever touched a drop of liquor."

"As we left," Fernando recalled, "I said, 'Father, what about that bag of coca leaves in your pocket?' At first he didn't want to part with it, but then he reached into his pocket and pulled out an enormous ball of coca and threw it into the gutter."

"I never looked back," Justiniano said.

Fernando leaned forward in his chair and reached for Rómulo's hand. He wanted the boy to understand the importance of his grandfather's conversion.

"Romi, you know we live and love and work together as a community—that is the Quechua way," Fernando said. "After your grandfather received the Lord in his heart, the entire family accepted the good news, and we all became believers in Jesus. And then little by little, other members of our community also came to believe in Him."

"It wasn't without cost," Grandfather said. "I remember some people came from other villages and threatened to burn down our house because of our new faith. The Catholic priest in one of the other villages stirred the people to violence. They would often stop your mother on the trail, Rómulo, and threaten to kill her children like frogs.

"They said, 'Those children have become little demons with horns and tails because you're following this new faith.' Zoila never fought back with words, although I know she wept many tears from the insults.

"Instead, your mother always prayed for these people, that God would forgive them. And she also prayed that God would raise up her sons to preach the gospel to these people who were insulting her," Grandfather concluded.

All the storytelling had exhausted Rómulo, and he could hardly keep his eyes open. Grandfather smoothed out the pillow and gently laid him down. "We'll continue this another time, little one, but it's time for you to sleep now."

Soon Rómulo was fast asleep. But Grandfather Justiniano and Fernando were in a talking mood. Moving closer to the fire, Justiniano looked across at his son with a father's admiring eye.

"Do you remember, Son, what happened that time we went to visit a pastor in Huanta?" Justiniano asked.

Fernando nodded. "That was when I was sixteen years old. The pastor said I should study at the Bible institute in his city."

"Yes," Justiniano continued, "I remember telling you that I believed he was right. I knew I would find a way to pay for your costs because this wasn't a game we were playing; it was about eternity."

"You know, Father, I had made up my mind that if you were willing to pay for my schooling, I would be ready to study. When we arrived back home, you gave me your white poncho and sent me on my way with your blessing. I was so happy as I took off on that two-day walk to Huanta."

Grandfather smiled. "Do you remember that little box of

Bible promises you gave me? They had different-colored cards with verses written on them, and you told me to read one before each meal. I did, and about two weeks later one of the cards I read had a verse from Joel 2:12, 'Even now return to me with all your heart, with fasting, weeping and mourning.'

"I turned to your grandmother and said, 'This is what the promise has told me, so today I'm going to fast and pray.' Right away she said, 'Perhaps Satan is using this little promise box to stop me. I was going to prepare that squash today to make *mazamorrita* (a Quechua dish). Can't you put off your fasting until another day and enjoy a bit of this first?'

"But I was firm. 'Even if I have to wait a year, there will still be squash,' I said. 'I'm going to fast today.' As I finished speaking these words, my belly began to churn, and seven bearded demons came out of my mouth."

Fernando laughed. "What? Are you sure, Father? How did you know they were demons?"

"I saw them with my own eyes, Fernando. That morning your mother took the goats out to pasture as the dawn was breaking. Instead of going to work in the fields, I took my little Bible and climbed up to this mountain where I read all day.

"When I came home that night, the others had already finished supper. The next morning I left at dawn again and came back just as the sun was setting. Everyone was eating dinner together, and your mother said, 'Enough of this fasting. You have already suffered two days of hunger. Here is your dinner—come and eat.'

"If she hadn't insisted, I'm sure I would have fasted for several more days. But after that period of prayer and fasting, the demons never came back. I never saw them again."

Fernando shook his head in amazement. "The Lord has done an amazing work in our family," he said softly. "It's almost incredible to me that our family continues to lead our people in the ways of God. So many of our brothers, sisters, and relatives have become pastors, teachers, and evangelists. It's as though our family was always meant to lead our people in the ways of the Creator—even as far back as Sacsayhuaman, when our forefathers led the spiritual worship in Cuzco so many centuries ago."

Justiniano nodded gravely but held his silence. All the reminiscing had tired him. He glanced over at the sleeping Rómulo and wondered what the future held in store for him. Would he too lead his people into the hope of the gospel? He prayed that God would choose little Rómulo, just as He had chosen so many others of the Quicaña clan, to carry the light of Jesus Christ through this dark world. God would answer that prayer beyond anything Justiniano could have asked or dreamed.

Rómulo's grandfather did much more than bring the good news about Jesus into his family. Soon after his conversion he became a leader in the community. He founded Chakiqpampa's first church, for there was no church at all until then, not even a Catholic chapel. Because Justiniano had come to the gospel through the witness of a Presbyterian pastor, the church in Chakiqpampa logically was Presbyterian. This would have repercussions as the community opened up to the world and came in contact with other Protestant traditions throughout the Andean hamlets of Ayacucho.

Together with Fernando, Justiniano began holding services in the small chapel he had built near his own home. The two would spend days visiting isolated communities, preaching the Word of God, and encouraging others to come to Christ. At first the people called them "devils" and "enemies." And sometimes they were driven out of the communities. But just as the Apostle Paul did so many centuries ago, Justiniano and Fernando counted it all joy.

In time the Quicaña father-and-son team organized several Presbyterian churches in the area. Soon more than fifty members of their extended family were following Christ. Two of Justiniano's daughters married ministers. These men also attended the Bible institute in Huanta where Fernando had studied. They began organizing churches throughout Peru, beyond their home province of Ayacucho. Just as Zoila, one of the first believers of Chakiqpampa, had prayed so long ago, the men and women of the Quicaña clan were preaching the gospel and making God's love known to the Quechua people.

One day Fernando came home early from a preaching trip and waited for his father to return from working in the fields. Fernando began to think about the many changes God had brought into their world. Something was troubling him. Finally Justiniano appeared.

"Father, what has the gospel of Jesus Christ done to our sense of *ayllu?*" Fernando blurted out. *Ayllu* was a driving force that held Quechua communities together, extending beyond family ties to encompass entire communities. It seemed to Fernando that the missionaries and their trained Peruvian pastors had presented the gospel as an individual relationship between God and man. This went against the the fabric of Quechua society and quietly subverted it.

The missionaries didn't seem to understand the concept of *ayllu* in the Quechua culture, nor did they encourage it. Although community festivals were often pagan affairs, those unfamiliar with Quechua culture failed sometimes to understand the importance of limited participation. Likewise, participation in community work projects was demanded of everyone, no matter their position or areas of responsibility. All members worked for one, and one worked for all. It was the Quechua way, but it was being threatened.

For some time now, the three communities that made up the municipality of Chakiqpampa—Kulluwanga, Viskacha, and Chakiqpampa proper—were embroiled in denominational divisions that threatened the very heart of their culture.

It began when a family from Kulluwanga traveled to Lima and learned about a Pentecostal church. When they returned several months later, they established a Pentecostal chapel. The services were significantly different from those of the Chakiqpampa Presbyterian Church. Members of each church began drawing distinctions between the two. And soon their differences divided them completely. The spirit of *ayllu* began to falter.

In time, a Seventh-Day Adventist church was founded in Viskacha, Chakiqpampa's third community. And with that the centuries of cohesiveness began to pull apart. New Christians weren't sure where they belonged and were easily influenced depending on whom they associated with. At one time the sharp sword of the gospel had brought enlightenment and hope. Now it seemed to grow more blunt with each passing year.

The missionaries encouraged new believers to internalize their faith, to move within the community of the church rather than the community at large. Through instructing Christians not to participate in community activities, the missionaries unwittingly robbed the new believers of an effective vehicle for sharing their faith in an atmosphere of *ayllu*.

Years later Fernando would deliver a major international address in which he blamed the division of his Quechua people on the way the gospel was first presented. But in the early years, the people depended completely on the missionaries and the Spanish church leadership. They had yet to develop a Quechua understanding of the good news of Jesus Christ. Nevertheless, Fernando conceded that the missionaries had sacrificially given of themselves that the Quechuas might know the Savior. And for that he would be eternally grateful.

Justiniano listened to Fernando's concerns and then encouraged him. "Son, what does it matter if someone is Presbyterian or Pentecostal? Someday we will transcend denominationalism, and there will be only one church—the Quechua church. Then we will truly regain *ayllu*, but it will be even better than before because we will all be centered in Jesus. I'm praying that God will grant us this blessing."

4

Move to the Corner of the Dead

U pon arriving in Lima, Rómulo Sauñe spent several days organizing the upcoming trip to Chakiqpampa. The journey would be a long one. After a flight to Ayacucho, a city in the Andean highlands southeast of Lima, there would be a truck ride deeper into Quechua territory and then a two-hour walk to his home village.

He thought of all his friends and neighbors and wanted to be sure no one was left out when he brought his gifts. That was Rómulo's trademark. His mind stopped at Luisa, a woman in Chosica whom he had encouraged. After she had died, Rómulo had often taken time out of his busy schedule to check on her children.

As Rómulo made final preparations for the flight to Ayacucho, he called in one of his colleagues and asked, "What happened to Luisa's son? Is he still around?" His colleague offered to look for the boy, but with few telephones in the homes of the transplanted Quechuas, it would be difficult to find him unless he happened to stop by. When Rómulo was in town, people seemed to gravitate to the Chosica Quechua center where Rómulo made his home.

A few days later Rómulo was going over some business matters. He looked up, and there was Luisa's son standing in the doorway, smiling shyly.

"Hey! There you are, Son. I've been looking for you," Rómulo exclaimed and ran to give him a hug. "Come in; let me look at you. How have you been?"

The little boy smiled broadly. His clothes were ragged, but his eyes sparkled at the attention.

"Will you stay for dinner?" Rómulo invited. "Of course you will. But first, let me show you what I brought you from my visit to the United States."

Rómulo reached for one of his travel bags and pulled out a brand new pair of green pants. "These look like they might be a perfect fit!"

The little boy trembled with excitement. "Oh, Rómulo, you remembered me."

"How could I ever forget you," Rómulo said softly as he hugged the boy. Then he prayed, "Lord, You are the Father of us all, but Your Word says You are particularly close to those without fathers and mothers. Be near to this boy. Bless his life and help him follow Your ways. Amen." Tears slid down the small boy's cheeks.

The following day Rómulo flew up to Ayacucho to begin the journey home. With great anticipation he made his way to Arcangel's house. Arcangel was away, but it didn't matter. Rómulo played with his little cousins and got reacquainted. When Arcangel finally strode in several hours later, the two warmly embraced, and then they went off to do some last-minute shopping. As Rómulo walked the familiar Ayacucho streets, it stirred deep memories of his early days in Chakiqpampa. More than once Rómulo glanced over at his proud uncle and friend and thought, *What would it have been like if my father had taken my family away from Chakiqpampa? Arca and I would never have known such good times together.*

At one point in his drifting about, Enrique Sauñe, Rómulo's father, found himself in jail. While he sat one evening reflecting on his wretched life, he pulled out a New Testament that his wife had given him. As he began to read, the Scriptures came alive, and his heart was broken. Tears streamed down his face as he came face to face with God's love and forgiveness. All the pride that had built up in his heart seemed to melt away. As he knelt down in the cell calling out to God, his heart was filled with a peace he had never known before.

Although he wasn't scheduled for release for quite some time, several days later the prison guards called him out of his cell and set him free. Elated, he walked out into the cobblestone street. God was already working in his life, just as Zoila had said He would. Enrique could hardly wait to get home and tell his wife what had happened. But without a penny to his name, it would be several weeks. He turned toward the highway out of town and began the trek that would eventually take him to a ministry extending throughout Peru and beyond—as an evangelist to the Quechua people. Perhaps if he had known this in the beginning, he might not have had the courage to set out. All his life he had taken the easy way. Now it was time to take the narrow road, the one that would lead him to the Savior.

Although Enrique had turned away from his godly heritage— his grandfather lived to preach his last sermon at 104—it was now just a matter of time before that desire to wander would be used by God to reach even the most remote hamlets where God's love was still unknown.

To Zoila's great joy, Enrique settled into life back in Chakiqpampa. He knew there was much to learn about Scripture. But life in Chakiqpampa was limited in many ways. So he made plans to move his family to the provincial capital of Ayacucho, a day's walk from the village. Perhaps there he could get some Bible training. But would the tug of the road be too much for him? Day and night he battled the urge to move on.

Finally Enrique packed his bags and was gone. By failing to see the family through the transition from Chakiqpampa to Ayacucho, he gave up any rightful authority as head of the household. There was no question in anyone's mind that the true head of the Sauñe-Quicaña clan was the patriarchal grandfather, Justiniano.

One day when Enrique drifted back into town from a trip to Lima, Grandfather Justiniano happened to be visiting the family. "What have you brought us from Lima?" Justiniano bellowed out.

Although well aware of the Quechua custom of bringing gifts, Enrique was not prepared. He began nervously to fish about in the old flour sack he used to carry his few belongings on his travels. Finally with great flourish he pulled out a small can of tuna fish and presented it to Justiniano.

"This is all you've brought us?" Justiniano cried out with fire in his eyes. "After five months of work in the capital, this is all you bring your family?" With a dramatic sweep of his hand, Justiniano pointed to the door. "Get out! You don't belong in this family!"

Enrique scooped up his belongings and ran for the door before Justiniano could physically throw him out. However, in the weeks that followed, Enrique often thought of the confrontation with his father-in-law. As he traveled around the country, his thoughts kept coming back to his responsibility to his family. During his last visit the children were dressed in rags. Some didn't even have shoes. He thought of Zoila and her pretty, shy smile. He loved to watch her work at her loom, making colorful blankets and tapestries to adorn their home.

He also felt an urge to preach the Word of God to his fellow Quechuas. It was time to put old things away and begin a new life. God would give him the strength to do it, he began to believe.

Meanwhile, Zoila continued to rise early in the morning well before dawn to pray for Enrique. All the children would gather round and remember their loved ones before the Lord. Zoila knew that prayer could accomplish anything, even bring a wayward husband home.

Several months later, it did. Enrique returned with a determination to succeed this time. As he joined in the family prayers, he sensed a new call on his life.

After the children had run off to school and the house quieted down, he turned to Zoila. "The Lord has called me to be an evangelist, Zoila," he began. "My heart aches for the Quechua people who still don't know of the love of God and His Son, Jesus. I know the Lord wants me to travel out to those seemingly forgotten villages to bring the message of His salvation. The Lord's army needs people like me to serve Him."

Zoila's heart leaped with joy. God had answered her prayers far above her highest hopes. But there was a lingering sadness. Once again, she knew, the family would be left alone for long stretches of time without any word of Enrique. There was a cost to serving the Lord, Zoila reminded herself. She was willing to pay that cost. How could she ever forget the first time she had heard the Word of God? Everyone needed to know of the Savior. Besides, she was a Quicaña, and the Quicañas came from a rich heritage of service. By giving Enrique to God's work, she would do her part in bringing others to Jesus Christ.

"You will know the truth and the truth will set you free." The words were hard for Justiniano to read in his Spanish Bible. Spanish was the language of the city—but it was not spoken in the Quicaña home. Millions of *Andinos*, or highland peoples of the Andean mountain range, spoke Quechua—in one of its many different dialects. It was the language of the Incas, the language that had prevailed over centuries to the present day. Justiniano's heart-language was Quechua.

After Justiniano's conversion to Christianity at the age of fifty, he spent many hours studying and reading the Bible. At that time it was only available in Spanish, so he painstakingly worked through the unfamiliar words. It was the only way to learn about his Creator and Lord. But once a concept had caught hold in his heart, Justiniano would pass this knowledge on to his congregation and especially to his family.

When Fernando Quicaña, his son, returned home from Bible school, Justiniano was proud of the knowledge he had gained. *There is nothing more sacred than to know God's Word,* he thought, *and now my son will lead others to the Lord with his knowledge.* Fernando had also learned something about Spanish culture, and this knowledge helped him mature and gain stature within the Quechua community.

Children were an integral part of the Quicaña family. Besides caring for his own children, Justiniano had overseen the education and training of his grandchildren when Enrique Sauñe was absent.

"You have royal blood, Rómulo," Grandfather Justiniano would tell his grandson as they sat on a craggy ledge overlooking a vast highland plain. Grandfather pointed out a thin line that crossed the plain and disappeared in a mountain pass. "Do you see that line, Rómulo?"

The little boy strained to see. "Do you mean that line like a path through the fields?"

"That's right, little one. It is a path. Many centuries ago the Incas built those footpaths for their royal messengers as they ran from city to city with important messages for the leaders of the empire. Some of those paths cut straight through huge boulders and high mountain passes. And when the messengers ran, they would get tired, so they chewed on some *coca* leaves for strength. I'm sure you've seen the big burlap bags filled with leaves for sale in the market."

Rómulo nodded and flashed a smile.

"Did you know, little one, that our ancestors once served The

Inca in Cuzco? Like the Levites of the Bible, our people carried out the priestly chores of the Inca nation," he reminded the boy. Rómulo sensed that his grandfather had chosen him to pass on the family history. And he listened carefully so he would not forget a single detail. Storytelling was an art form among his people, for there had never been a written language to record what had happened over the centuries. The older generation passed the stories along to the younger generation.

Grandfather put his arm around his young grandson and smiled kindly. "I've told you some wonderful stories about our past, haven't I, little Romi? But the best stories ever told are in this book." He pointed to his well-worn Spanish Bible in the bag next to him. "My only regret is that I didn't learn to read earlier and study more as a child."

As Justiniano spoke, an idea developed in his mind that would change the course of his family's history. Rather than herd goats and sheep all day, Rómulo should see the world and bring some of it back for the good of their people. Over the next few days Justiniano toyed with the idea and how to accomplish it.

One evening as his wife served dinner, Justiniano announced, "Ignorance will end with my generation. If you are all willing to study," he said looking at the children, "I will help each of you get an education."

At ten years of age, Rómulo was ready for the challenge. He was frustrated by his lack of ability in the classroom, but perhaps somewhere else there was hope for him. *Oh, to be able to study with other children and to understand the lessons,* he thought to himself. Maybe then he would shed the awful nickname of *Opa* or Dumb One.

Though Justiniano had no reason to believe Rómulo would do better in a new educational environment, he knew the boy had a big heart and a gentle spirit. Whatever was standing in his way, he would find a way to overcome it. His willingness to listen, to obey, and to find solutions were leadership qualities that needed honing.

"You'll get your chance to learn, Rómulo," he encouraged. "We'll find it for you in Ayacucho; you'll see."

While life in Chakiqpampa was peaceful and safe, there was little opportunity for anything more than a grammar school education. When Enrique returned to the family, he agreed with Justiniano that there were far more opportunities for work and an education in the city of Ayacucho. After the family talked it over, it was agreed that Zoila, her children, and her brother Arcangel would move to the city.

Grandfather Quicaña and the older boys worked out all the plans. They bought a small piece of land in Ayacucho—the capital of the department or province of Ayacucho—and began building a modest little house. Piece by piece, they carried all the materials they needed from Chakiqpampa. Back home such a house would have been a respectable dwelling, but in Ayacucho it was a dismal affair. Still the prospects of living in the city raised their spirits, and no one noticed that the house was located in the poorest neighborhood of the city.

After the family was settled in, Justiniano and Teofila returned to Chakiqpampa, leaving Zoila in charge. Because Arcangel, her brother, was just a young boy, he would stay with her and also go to school. Arcangel and Rómulo were glad they would not be separated. Here in the city they would figure things out together and learn how to cope with all the strange customs.

The first few months in Ayacucho were eye openers for the boys. They had never seen cars or pavement on the streets. Each day held new learning experiences. But life was hard and the family struggled to provide even the most basic necessities.

One day Zoila could think of no other solution to increase the family income than to place Rómulo in the service of a Spanish family, where at least he would get something to eat and a place to sleep. They would also pay a small wage. She was reluctant to put him in such an unfamiliar environment, but the pressure of poverty forced her. Somehow little Romi would find a way to survive.

The appointed day finally arrived, and Zoila took Rómulo to the home of the wealthy Spanish family. A maid whisked him in the back door and sat him down in the kitchen. The bewildered boy could hardly stop staring, his mouth agape at all the wonderful things. The maid tried to explain something to him, but Rómulo didn't understand. *How was he ever going to do his job?* he wondered. Tears welled up in his eyes. He wanted to go home, but his family needed him to be a man and earn a living. He would do his best.

"Rómulo," the maid said, "I'm going to teach you how to sweep the floor because that will be your job." She handed him the broom and showed him where to begin sweeping. Rómulo just stood there. Finally the maid realized that Rómulo didn't understand. *Oh my, another country boy,* she thought. She took the broom and began to sweep the kitchen floor. Then she opened the back door and swept the dust out onto the ground. Pointing at Rómulo, she handed the broom back to him and then gave him a little shove. Finally he got the idea.

The maid knew this was one of the easier chores that would fall into Rómulo's lap. How she was going to communicate the more complicated ones was beyond her. Maybe the *jefe*, or man of the house, didn't know Rómulo couldn't speak Spanish. Well, he would soon find out, and then it would be his problem.

After dinner the maid showed Rómulo where he would sleep. But before going to bed, Rómulo knew he would need to go to the bathroom. What to do? The maid showed him a room with pretty white porcelain, but he didn't know what that was for. As the minutes ticked by, he became almost panic-stricken. Where could he go? At home he just walked out into the field behind the house, but here there were no fields. Finally there was nothing else to do except to run outside. He raced out to the sidewalk and down the street where he found relief behind a tree. But what would the *jefe* say? Oh, this world was too much trouble. If only they could all go back to Chakiqpampa.

Life in the Spanish household *was* complicated and often incomprehensible. He began learning Spanish words and understanding instructions, but here he was just an Indian, and rarely did anyone have a kind thing to say to him. Each night he cried himself to sleep, lonely for his mother and Arcangel. Early one morning he made up his mind that he wouldn't live another day in that house. He slipped out the back door and ran away. He would never forget the frustration and terror of being a stranger in a foreign place. And his heart would never stop hurting for the thousands of Quechuas forced to seek work in the Spanish cities and in the dislocation find themselves the lowest members of the social strata.

One day not long after Rómulo returned home, he and Arcangel were walking down the street and talking. "Arca, what will we do here in Ayacucho? How will we live?"

"Maybe we could sell newspapers on the street," Arcangel mused. "But I don't know how to go about it."

"We'll find out," Rómulo said. "But do you think they will mind if I don't have any shoes?"

"I don't think so, Rómulo," Arcangel replied. "Look at all the other boys; most of them don't have shoes either."

Rómulo approached a boy selling newspapers outside a restaurant and asked him where his boss was.

"Down the street," he said, pointing out an imposing structure with a guard posted outside. "Luis Sanchez is in charge of all the newspaper boys."

As they neared the office, Rómulo and Arcangel carefully tucked in their worn shirts and finger-combed their hair. Zoila would be proud of them if they could get a job. And the thought of it gave them confidence. After a short chat, Mr. Sanchez told the boys they were hired and explained to them where their territory would be. "Don't go anywhere else," he warned, "or one of the older newspaper boys might fight you for the territory." Then he showed them where to collect each day's supply of newspapers.

The next step was to purchase a shoeshine kit. Newspapers would be sold out by noon, but shoes could be shined all day. So after a few weeks of peddling newspapers, the boys pooled their money and bought a makeshift shoeshine kit for a few pennies at the Saturday market. Before long, Arcangel and Rómulo were into their new routine as newspaper boys in the morning and shoe-shiners in the afternoon. Each evening as they returned home, they stopped off at a corner bakery and bought bread for the family with their day's earnings. But Zoila didn't get all of their money. Whenever they thought they could get away with it, the boys kept a few pennies back from their weekly earnings so they could go to the movies with the other boys.

One day as Rómulo was selling newspapers on the street, a man walked up to him and smiled. "Hello," he offered and extended his hand to Rómulo. Spanish men often treated the boy rudely. Not used to such attention, Rómulo shyly looked up but kept his hands in his pockets.

"Hello," he answered.

"I've been watching you sell newspapers on this corner every day while all the children are in school. Why aren't you in school, Son?" he asked.

"I've been to school," Rómulo answered, "but I could never learn anything. It was too difficult. I didn't understand Spanish."

"But your Spanish has improved," the man said with an encouraging tone in his voice. "You should be learning to read and write like all the other children."

Rómulo only nodded. He very much wanted to go, but what if he still couldn't learn? He would have to start from the beginning, and he was so much older than the rest of the children in the grammar school.

As if reading his mind, the man smiled and said, "You're a little old to be starting first grade, but don't worry about that. I'll be there to help you. Whenever you have a problem, you can come to see me. You see, I'm a teacher at the school, and I know from seeing how well you sell these newspapers and shine the shoes that you're bright and you can do the work. Will you come to school tomorrow? I'll wait for you out front."

Rómulo smiled brightly at the schoolteacher. How could this man know how much he wanted to study, to learn with the other children, and to make something of himself? This was why Grandfather Justiniano had brought him here to the city. But in the struggle to survive, Mother had forgotten to see to his education.

Rómulo glanced at the stranger and murmured, "I'd like to come. I'll ask my father if I can." Then with a wave he raced off toward home.

That night Enrique listened as Rómulo excitedly described the encounter with the schoolteacher. "Rómulo, if you want to go to school, it's fine with me, but you'll have to buy your own school supplies. We don't have any money for that," he said with finality. He hoped Rómulo wouldn't be disappointed if he didn't do well in school.

Rómulo's heart was filled with excitement. Finally—a chance to learn with the other children. Who was that wonderful man who spoke with him? Why would he care about a newspaper boy? Romulo's hands were stained with black shoe wax, and his clothes were ragged and patched. He didn't even have a pair of shoes. Would the other children laugh at him? Defiantly he said to himself, "I don't care. I'm going to learn, and that teacher is going to help me."

Several months later Rómulo and Arcangel were on their way home from a day of selling newspapers and shining shoes.

Rómulo was troubled. "Arcangel, have you noticed how rough the other boys are? They use such foul language. And they steal from each other, and they don't even care that it's not right. This isn't how we were taught back in Chakiqpampa."

"Maybe we're in the wrong job, Rómulo," Arcangel suggested. "Is there another way we can earn some money?"

After asking around, the boys learned of a local baker who needed help. Soon Rómulo and Arcangel began working near the bakery's hot ovens throughout the night. The bakers would start making the bread in the middle of the night so that it would be fresh for the customers at first light. The best part of the job was that the manager let them each bring home a bag of bread after the work was done.

In the afternoon they were expected to clean out the ovens. Arcangel and Rómulo scavenged the fields in the countryside where they collected a special type of leaf the locals used for such chores. With a large load of these leaves, they returned to the city and whatever was left over from their job they sold in the streets. Little by little the boys were learning to make their way in the world of the Spanish.

Music was Rómulo's passion. From the days when he had played his *quena* while he watched over his flocks in the fields, he had turned to music to lift his spirits. One day when Rómulo was a teenager, his mother sent him to the bakery to purchase the family's daily supply of bread. As he approached the bakery, the neighborhood drunk called out to him, "If you give me your bread money, I'll sell you my guitar."

Rómulo examined the handmade guitar. "It's a deal," he said, without thinking twice.

Minutes later Rómulo arrived back home anxious to show off his guitar. He had completely forgotten his errand. Spying Arcangel by the shed, he held out his new guitar.

"Who sold you this, Rómulo?" Arcangel laughed. "It must have been some peasant who didn't know the first thing about the craftsmanship and skill it takes to make these instruments. It's worthless!"

Rómulo was speechless. "What do we do now?"

"Well, why did you buy it?"

"To play it," Rómulo answered. Then to escape his dilemma, he offered, "Here. The guitar is yours."

Arcangel took the guitar and with it the challenge of explaining to his sister Zoila what had happened to her bread. Arcangel's parents Justiniano and Teofila were visiting from Chakiqpampa. Maybe they would know what to do.

Justiniano chuckled. "Here's some money," he said reaching into his pocket. "Go buy the bread, and let's say nothing more about it."

Arcangel and Rómulo joyfully ran off to the bakery.

As in Chakiqpampa, the church remained the central focus of family life. They began to attend a small Presbyterian church in Ayacucho called La Libertad, or Liberty. Unlike most of the churches in Ayacucho, the services at the La Libertad church were in Quechua instead of Spanish. Situated on a hillside in the poverty-stricken neighborhood where many Quechuas ended up after moving to Ayacucho, the church was filled with evangelicals from the surrounding area. Many in the congregation came from Chakiqpampa, bringing a sense of community to the new migrants. For all of the transplanted members, life in Ayacucho had brought culture shock. But it was worth it. Now they worked for themselves rather than for the landowners. They were free!

As the years passed, the La Libertad church prospered. The sign over the entrance proclaiming, "The truth will set you free," symbolized the revolutionary step these people took in bringing their culture to Ayacucho. They were setting off their own revolution through the gospel of Jesus Christ. In a similar fashion across town at the university, the Marxist-influenced professors were beginning to indoctrinate their students with a new ideology.

At the La Libertad church, however, young men like Rómulo and Arcangel were learning a strong, pure gospel far more appealing than any man-made ideologies they encountered in Spanish society. Rómulo taught the twelve-year-old boys the lessons he had learned at his grandfather's feet, and his leadership in the church deeply affected the younger boys' lives.

Rómulo always incorporated music into his lessons. He held his class spellbound as he told stories from the Bible or taught them new songs from Scripture.

One day Rómulo taught them a new song from Psalm 100. "This song has a repeated line: 'For the Lord is good and His love endures forever,'" Rómulo instructed them. "When you're going through any sort of difficulty, maybe learning Spanish, or struggling with a problem in your family, or finding a job that pays enough, isn't it good to know that in the middle of it all the Lord still loves us and His goodness endures forever."

The boys nodded knowingly. "There's more to the song, but let's just try this first part: 'For the Lord is good and His love endures forever.'" After several repetitions the room rang with the words of this ageless Psalm. Then Rómulo continued, "And the next part of it is 'His faithfulness continues through all generations.'"

After they sang through the entire verse several times, Rómulo said, "Some of you have brothers and sisters and parents who don't know the Lord. Isn't it a blessing to know that although people disappoint you and are unfaithful, the Lord is faithful throughout all generations? What promises of reassurance and hope!"

So Rómulo taught the young Quechuas to find inspiration and encouragement from the Scriptures.

5

So Mother Can Understand It

The marketplace bustled with activity. Rómulo and Arcangel slowly made their way through stalls of fruits and vegetables—and highlanders selling small bags of coca leaves which they scooped out of large burlap bags. It seemed that at every turn Rómulo bumped into an old friend or an acquaintance. The familiarity of it all energized him. To everyone he met, Rómulo proudly told his plan to return to his childhood home in Chakiqpampa. "I'm going back to my roots," he exclaimed, "and to pay my respects at my grandfather's grave." And his friends responded with great enthusiasm.

In a small bag he had left back at Arcangel's house, Rómulo kept his treasured Quechua Bible. How he wished he had brought a few extra copies with him. Some of his old friends and acquaintances still did not know his Lord.

Life in Ayacucho was difficult. Each day brought news of another terrorist attack or a military raid. There were always deaths. And refugees kept streaming into the city seeking food and shelter. Rómulo's heart bled for these dear people. Who would care for them? Who but the Lord could understand the fear in their hearts? He made a mental note to speak to his colleagues in Ayacucho about distributing more Bibles in the city and up in the mountain communities.

With each old friend they came across, Arcangel could see that Rómulo was already beginning to relive the past. His excitement was infectious, and by the time they were finished shopping, everyone knew that they were on their way to Chakiqpampa. The usually wary and reserved Arcangel said nothing, but he worried about Rómulo's openness. These were not the times to be telling everyone your business. But that was Rómulo. He let Arcangel do all the worrying. And that's how it always seemed to be.

A busy hub of activity, the bilingual training school in Ayacucho saw each day the comings and goings of colorfully dressed Quechua men and women, wearing characteristic fedora-like hats. Many of the women brought their babies along, tied snugly into multicolored swaths of cloth anchored firmly around their shoulders.

In the training center they learned to read and write in both Spanish and Quechua—in a program that would eventually reach tens of thousands of Quechuas. Each year Fernando Quicaña, who had taken over its leadership, invited dozens of Quechua church leaders, laymen and laywomen, to study there. The center played an important part in Wycliffe Bible Translators' program to provide education to the Quechuas.

The bilingual school was located on the outskirts of Ayacucho in the community of Quicapata. In this idyllic location students could study without the distractions of the city, surrounded by well-kept gardens and instructors who wished them well. It was a period of relative peace in the life of the Quicaña-Sauñe clan. Enrique Sauñe's return to the family had brought a sense of stability to their life in Ayacucho. In time he took the job of caretaker at the Quicapata center, and soon the family moved into the caretaker's home on the grounds. Although Enrique continued to travel as an itinerant evangelist, when he was gone, the family felt safe and secure.

Rómulo and Arcangel worked as groundskeepers, planting flowers, mowing the lawns, and attending to the upkeep of the buildings.

Conrad Phelps, a newly arrived translator who hoped to work on the Ayacucho dialect of the Quechua New Testament, often struck up conversations with the teenagers to practice his Quechua. One day Conrad happened to mention that a certain lady named Irma was coming to visit. Irma was from Cuzco!

Rómulo and Arcangel talked about the impending visit with great anticipation. Visits by Quechuas from Cuzco were a novelty. The Cuzco Quechua dialect had some differences and nuances that the Ayacucho Quechuas couldn't understand. Irma, Conrad had told them, was part Quechua. Little did Rómulo know that in the years ahead, Conrad and Irma would become like a second family to him. Within a year Conrad and Irma were married.

Since the late 1950s, the Quechuas of Ayacucho had had a New Testament in their dialect. But Bible translation techniques were still in their infancy, and the translation turned out to be too literal.

One day Fernando Quicaña and several other Presbyterian church leaders approached one of the translators, Homer Emerson, with the dilemma.

"We've been trying to read the Quechua Scriptures, Brother Homer," Fernando began, "but we've had a hard time making sense of them."

Another leader chimed in, "Yes, some of the stories don't make sense to us as they've been translated. It makes it difficult to memorize and read aloud."

Homer had invested many years in translating the Scriptures

for the Quechuas. Their frankness was painful to hear, and he remained silent.

The young men didn't really get their point across to Homer, but they kept hoping for a new translation. By the early 1970s, it was clear that a simpler, more idiomatic New Testament was needed for the Ayacucho Quechuas. Wycliffe assigned missionaries Conrad and Irma Phelps to begin the translation. In the process of learning Ayacucho Quechua, Conrad began to collect stories and folk tales to get a better feel for the language and its expressions. Among those who taped anecdotes for Conrad were the men of the Quicaña-Sauñe family—Justiniano, Fernando, and even Rómulo.

When the team needed a language helper, the choice was easy—Rómulo Sauñe. His quick wit, his love for his people, and his ability to guide them through the intricacies of the Quechua language made him a crucial member. The team finally took on the cohesiveness Conrad had been searching for.

Over the course of that first year the Phelpses lived and worked in a number of different Quechua villages as they learned the language and became familiar with the culture. In one village they decided to visit every household. Soon the people got used to seeing them as they walked about.

"They assumed we didn't understand them when they talked with each other," Conrad recalled. "So they felt free to talk about anything—like their fear of death or their beliefs in the spirit of the ground. We learned about how they would dedicate some of their animals to the spirit of the mountains to prevent them from breaking their legs as they traversed the mountain trails."

With the introduction to Bible translation work, Rómulo's world began to expand. Although during the week he attended high school, the weekends were filled with new concepts and experiences. Every Saturday he came to the Phelps' home eager to be part of this exciting new work he was only beginning to understand. In the mornings Rómulo and Irma worked together at translating Mark's Gospel. In the afternoon, Rómulo worked with Conrad on the translation of the Acts of the Apostles.

From the first weeks of work, Conrad knew Rómulo was especially gifted in translation work. Instead of approaching the task word for word, which had proven to be an ineffective technique, Rómulo translated from idea to idea.

"Here's the Spanish," Conrad would say as he read the selected verse. After a moment of thought, Rómulo would offer, "We can say that in Quechua . . ."

Conrad was often amazed at the fluid way Rómulo could process even the most complicated phrases. It was rare to meet a native Quechua speaker whose grasp of the Spanish language enabled him to freely translate the concepts and grammatical structures from the Spanish into his native tongue. Even though the work was often laborious and mechanical, Rómulo rarely grew weary. Instead he would plead with Conrad, "Can't we work a little longer?" or "May I take some of the work home with me?"

But Rómulo's motivation did not seem to be rooted solely in the act of learning a new skill and applying it to his own life; he worked with an urgency that mystified Conrad.

One day Conrad leaned back in his chair and studied Rómulo. The two were surrounded by commentaries, Bibles, and reference books—a scene of intellectual effort familiar to Conrad but seemingly out of character for a teenager, or so Conrad thought.

"Rómulo, why is this work so important to you?"

Rómulo looked up and smiled. He motioned Conrad to the window and pointed to a group of Quechua women chatting in the distance.

"See those women over there? Any one of them could be my mother," he told Conrad. "My mother never really learned to speak Spanish, although she understands much of it. But even though my mother loves the Lord, she will never be able to understand all that God wants her to know because she doesn't hear the words in her own language. That's why translating God's Word has such urgency for me."

The fire in Rómulo's spirit and his devotion to the work also motivated the Phelpses, even though they knew that many translators worked for decades to complete just the New Testament in an indigenous language. Rómulo wanted the whole Bible in his own language, and he wanted it *now*.

One morning as Rómulo and Irma worked on the book of Mark, Irma went back and forth between English translation manuals and Spanish commentaries. Understanding the passage was the first step of translation. Once that was clear, Rómulo would begin to suggest possible phrasing in Quechua. He was frustrated that he couldn't read about the theories and techniques of translation but had to rely totally on Irma's explanations.

"Oh, why are all these books about translation in English?" he blurted out. "Why can't I read them in Spanish?"

"Rómulo," Irma said patiently, "these books aren't in Spanish yet because it's only been in the last few years that these techniques were invented. These books are new in English."

"Then I'll have to learn English," Rómulo said with determination. "You'll have to teach me. How soon can we start?"

Irma laughed. "Rómulo, we've got to keep going on the Gospel of Mark. We'll have to see about learning English."

In the following weeks Rómulo was especially attentive when Conrad and Irma discussed the work. Often they would switch between Spanish and English as they struggled with a certain passage.

"Honey," Irma would ask, "how would you explain *transformed* in Quechua?"

Or she would call out from another room, "Honey, how would you approach a translation of 'saving the best wine until last' in Quechua?"

Rómulo silently mouthed the English word that she often repeated before a sentence—*Honey*.

One day Rómulo approached Conrad with a problem. Here was his chance to practice his new English word, "Honey," he began, "where is the section we worked on yesterday?" Conrad stared at Rómulo. Irma was walking by and stopped in her tracks. "Rómulo, why are you calling Conrad 'Honey'?"

"You always call him 'Honey' when you come to him with a problem. I wanted to try out my English."

"But, Rómulo," Irma explained, "'Honey' is an affectionate name I use with Conrad. It means *miel* (Spanish for honey)."

Rómulo burst out laughing, and Conrad and Irma joined in. "Someday when I get myself a wife, I'm going to call *her* Honey."

Rather than hide his Quechua roots, Rómulo proudly displayed them in the telling of stories from his childhood. One beautiful spring day Irma and Rómulo took a break from the translation work. They were sitting outside under a tree.

"You know, Irma, from a young age we Quechuas are taught to be brave. We're told we have to endure pain and not cry. Sometimes a father takes his young son by the hand and forces him to place it in an ant's nest. When the fire ants start to bite and sting, the child isn't allowed to remove his hand or to cry. He just has to endure it. That's how we're taught to withstand the harshness of our life in the mountains."

Irma nodded with interest. Suddenly she noticed Rómulo's hand. It was covered with fire ants. He had deliberately placed it over a mound of ants. "Rómulo," she cried in alarm, "what are you doing! Get those ants off!"

"Oh, Irma, this is nothing. I just wanted to show you how our parents teach us to be brave." Then he brushed the ants off his arm, revealing a number of swelling welts where the ants had stung him.

In the course of the translation work, it was often necessary to travel to Quechua villages to test a newly translated section of Scripture. If Conrad was away, Irma would drive the Jeep, and Rómulo would direct the way. Every time they went on a long trip into the mountains, Rómulo would pester Irma for a chance to drive. He had watched Conrad and Irma drive for quite some time, and he thought he knew what to do.

"Please, Irma, let me drive," he playfully repeated over and over again.

"But, Rómulo," Irma countered, "you can't drive."

Still he kept asking.

One day as they drove back from a visit to a distant village, Irma felt tired. She was expecting another baby soon, and she was weary from the long day.

Rómulo gave her a searching look. "Irma, could I drive?"

"Okay," she said. And they switched seats.

Rómulo gave the clutch a try and then sampled the brakes. Finally he turned on the ignition and eased the Jeep into gear. Then much to Irma's surprise, Rómulo vigorously plunged his foot onto the accelerator, and the Jeep sped off down the highway. Irma hung onto the dashboard trying to hold back a scream. Finally as the Jeep approached a sharp curve, Irma shouted, "Stop!"

Immediately Rómulo eased off the gas and began slowing down. With a jerk and a stall, the Jeep rolled to the side and came to a halt. At first Rómulo couldn't release his grip on the steering wheel, but in a moment he turned to Irma and said, "Now I'm not afraid of driving." And he promptly got out of the car and walked around to the passenger side. Irma slid across the seat, amazed and surprised at Rómulo's eagerness to conquer what had apparently been a hidden fear.

The initial learning disabilities which had delayed Rómulo's education were now far behind him, and he was at the top of his high school class. The importance of finishing high school as the top student was crucial, for any student who graduated first in his class was entitled to attend the university of his choice. This important fact was not lost on Rómulo.

One day Rómulo appeared at the Phelpses' home troubled and discouraged. He had a difficult time concentrating on the work, and finally Conrad asked, "Is something bothering you, Rómulo?"

"Yes, I'm worried about my school grades. It's not that I haven't done well, but lately I've been arguing with my teachers, and I think this will hurt my academic standing."

In the 1970s Ayacucho was a hotbed of Communist liberal thought. The growing Marxist influence at the University of Huamanga was beginning to trickle down into the local high schools. Each crop of teachers who graduated from the university brought with them strong Marxist ideas. They worked evolutionary and Marxist ideals into everything they taught, even geography or mathematics lessons. The entire direction of the instruction disheartened Rómulo. Day after day he had to sift through the material in his classes and sort out the Marxism. The process was laborious and ultimately depressing.

"I can't stand the brainwashing of the students," Rómulo told Conrad. "I've been challenging the teachers on their points using my Bible as a reference. It's not winning me any popularity contests with the teachers."

In fact, the teachers had marked Rómulo as a troublemaker— someone to keep a careful eye on.

"There's such a feeling of despair here among the young people," Rómulo said. "The only way to get ahead is through the university, and the university is full of Marxism. And now it's not just in the university, but it's coming into the high schools and even the grade schools."

Rómulo doubled his resolve to defend the cause of Christ in the midst of such oppression. He asked Conrad to help him develop arguments to use in his discussions with his teachers. Besides the help he received from the Phelpses, Rómulo sat in on meetings held by Christian students at the university. He was about their age, but because his education had been delayed for several years, his studies were still at the high school level. He enjoyed accompanying Arcangel to the University Bible Circle meetings, but he didn't participate.

As the ideological debates became more heated, the discussions grew more interesting. Sometimes a student activist came to try to intimidate the Christian students. Rómulo would whisper to Arcangel, who was a member of the university group, "Tell him this or tell him that." Rómulo drew on the arguments Conrad had helped him develop.

In time the Marxist activists became less confrontational. But sometimes the debates reached such a theoretical level that Arcangel and Rómulo would slip out the back door shaking their heads. They wanted to understand, but it was too difficult.

The university Bible study group often took field trips around the country where they would hold retreats, and Rómulo was always invited to come along. One weekend the group traveled down to the coast, to a stretch of beach just north of Lima. When Rómulo got off the chartered bus, he rushed to the beach along with the others. Suddenly the vastness of the ocean came into view, and he stood on a small bluff transfixed, the salted breeze blowing through his hair.

The days passed like a dream. Everything was new and different. At night his friends sat around the campfire singing songs and telling funny stories. Each night someone happened to mention the presence of El Frontón, a prison out in the sea, so they said.

Rómulo didn't want to appear ignorant, but the thought of a prison in the sea gnawed at him as the others joked and played their games on the beach. Sometimes he would pause and stare out into the fog and wonder, "How could a prison be in the sea?"

One day the group took an excursion up the coast where they said they would be able to see the prison. The thought of it excited Rómulo. This would certainly be something to talk about back home. No one there had ever seen the ocean, much less a prison inside it.

Eagerly he ran with the others to the shore where waves gently lapped against the beach. Someone yelled out, "Look! There's El Frontón!"

Rómulo strained to see where they were pointing. All he could make out was the faint outline of an island in the middle of a swirling fog.

"I don't see anything," he said.

A friend threw an arm around his shoulder and helped line up his vision with the place he was pointing out for him.

"There. That's El Frontón. Don't you see it?"

Suddenly it struck Rómulo—the prison was on an island, not in the sea. After a long pause, he sputtered, "But . . . you deceived me. You said the prison was in the sea."

"We didn't mislead you, Rómulo," they laughed. "The prison isn't *in* the sea, but it is *at* sea. It's an island in the ocean."

A bit embarrassed, Rómulo laughed with everyone else at his mistake.

Rómulo's ability to laugh at himself was a unique quality. More often than not, an indigenous person would not want to make any mistakes that would cause him to lose face in the Spanish culture. Native Indians already faced so many cultural prejudices that to reinforce longstanding beliefs that Indians were basically illiterate simpletons was painful.

On the other hand, because of cultural prejudice and the division between *mestizos* and native Indians, Spanish culture often overlooked the Quechuas' wonderful sense of playfulness. No one showed this love for fun more than Rómulo. Perhaps it helped to have a lifelong friend and ally in Arcangel. The harshness of their childhood, the deprivations of life in the remote hamlets that dot the Andes, had not tempered Rómulo's jovial spirit.

As Rómulo's world began to spread beyond Ayacucho, he was becoming more familiar with Spanish culture. There was so much to learn, and no one was more eager. One day Arcangel suggested to Rómulo that they go to the jungle. Peru boasts three radically different climates. The coast is a series of rolling hills dotted with scrub brush and small dusty villages. Even Lima, the capital, rarely experiences rainfall, and everything is covered with a thin layer of dust.

The mighty Andean mountain chain, stretching the entire length of the continent, transects the heart of Peru. Here Rómulo grew up, and here the Quechua people are predominant. At the high altitudes, the weather is like an eternal spring. On the eastern slope of the mountain range lies a thick jungle, not unlike that portrayed in the Tarzan movies the boys saw in Ayacucho's theater.

Arcangel suggested that they bring along Luisa and Juanita from the University Bible Circle. "It will be an adventure," he said with a playful chuckle. As always, Rómulo was ready for adventure.

The following weekend, Rómulo and Arcangel set off with the two young women on the bus to Huanta. The bus dropped them off on the outskirts at a restaurant where they planned to have lunch. All four shed their heavy sweaters. The humidity was foreign to them, but soon they were ready for the jungle. The air was full of the sound of screeching and cawing and hooting and howling. The rain forest seemed to have a life of its own, its brightly colored flowers like a pretty girl's earrings sparkling in the sun.

Arcangel discovered a path that led through a thick canopy to a nearby stream. As they walked, Rómulo and Arcangel entertained Luisa and Juanita with stories of their childhood. Arcangel led the way and Rómulo trailed behind. Suddenly Rómulo had a brilliant idea. When the others were not looking, he broke away and circled through the jungle until he was far ahead of them. Then as they approached, he reached up for a long vine and swung out over the trail with a mighty Tarzan yell, "Ayi-yah-i-yah!"

At the zenith of the swing, the vine broke, and Rómulo tumbled down, falling flat on his back into a mud puddle with a loud whump! The three stood speechless as Rómulo struggled to regain his breath. Then they all exploded into laughter, leaning weakly against the trees.

Rómulo got back on his feet and flashed a big smile. "Surprised?"

6

Love and Avocados

If we take anything else, we won't have room for all the people," Arcangel complained, as he and Rómulo packed the back of the pickup. "And you have to stop inviting more people to come along with us. We don't really even know some of those you've invited. It's a good thing most of them have turned you down." Arcangel had just returned from a long trip to Ecuador, and he was tired. All the stuff they were packing into the truck would have to be carried in to the village because there was no other way to get to their home.

Rómulo sensed Arcangel's frustration. "Look, Arcangel, do you remember how we loved it when people brought us candy from the city?" Rómulo reached over and touched the big bags of cookies and candy he had purchased in the marketplace that morning. "The children in Chakiqpampa will squeal with delight to have such a treat. If we leave this all behind, they will feel left out. They care much more about this than they do about a new shirt or a new sweater. Isn't that so, Arcangel?"

Arcangel nodded. "You win, Rómulo. You always do because I can't argue with your logic. All right, load it all up, and let's move because it's getting late."

While Rómulo and Arcangel were loading the truck, Zoila and a family friend, Margarita Fajardo, were on an important errand. Zoila wore the traditional white hat distinctive of the Quechua women from Chakiqpampa. She was slightly built, but her physical and inner strength made her seem tall. She and Margarita had been charged with assembling the makings of a big barbecue that Rómulo planned for the village. Margarita and her husband Alfredo were very close to Rómulo and the Sauñe-Quicaña clan, ever since Rómulo had led Alfredo to the Lord more than ten years before. Margarita was a sensitive and pretty young woman who always kept an eye out for someone with a need. Now she and Zoila hunted through the marketplace for herbs and spices.

Soon they were on their way to Arcangel's house loaded down with their important purchases. Rómulo had promised a feast of celebration—and it would be centered around the Quechua-style barbecue known as a *pachamanca*. The pachamancas were a tradition among the Quechua people, and no one had put one on with more flourish than Grandfather Justiniano during his heyday. Rómulo wanted to model all that he loved about his grandfather. Once they were all together, like his grandfather, Rómulo planned to talk to them about the Lord Jesus. Ever since the war had invaded their lives and destroyed much of the communal lifestyle, the pachamancas were few and far between.

"Too bad Donna didn't come on this trip," Margarita remarked, as she helped Rómulo load the truck. "It would have been fun to see her again. She would have loved shopping with us in the market today."

Donna. Rómulo's heart beat a little faster. His blonde-haired American wife. Donna and the four Sauñe children were back in the United States with Donna's parents, Art and Dorothy Jackson, Wycliffe missionaries to Peru.

Rómulo's family was always in his thoughts. He was glad that they had an opportunity to relax in the States for a few months. It was important for the grandparents to get to know their

Peruvian grandchildren, and it was good for Donna to be with her own family. Now as he packed a bag full of fruits and vegetables, Margarita's chatter reminded him of how he had first met Donna.

The brown waters of the lake lapped against the lush shoreline as the gentle sound of "pecky pecky" filled the air. The sound came from outboard motors attached to large mahogany canoes carrying people and goods from one side of Lake Yarinacocha to the other.

A Wycliffe Bible Translators translation center nestled along one section of the lake. Here missionaries lived in tin-roofed houses with screens instead of windows. The nearest town, Pucallpa, was a few miles away.

For months Rómulo had been working day in and day out with Conrad and Irma Phelps on the New Testament translation. Now they had come to Yarinacocha to deal with some of the final segments. For most of the day the trio worked in air-conditioned study rooms, or "cool rooms."

The days sweltered with heat and humidity. Even area residents dripped with perspiration. For Rómulo, accustomed to the temperate mountain climate, the mugginess of the rain forest was almost unbearable. One afternoon the Phelps called for a break, and Rómulo headed off to the lake for a swim with his Peruvian friends.

As they arrived at the beach, they saw several girls already in the water. Rómulo immediately recognized them as the daughters of the missionaries he had met while working at the center. He and the others soon joined in the fun, swimming out to a platform bobbing up and down on the waves a short distance away. Just to impress the girls, they would crawl up and perform wild dives head first, feet first, tumbling in with a hop, skip, and a jump—whatever they thought would get the girls' attention.

Rómulo was particularly drawn to one fair-haired young woman with pretty blue eyes. Gathering his courage, he introduced himself to her and learned that her name was Donna Jackson. Although born in the States, Donna considered herself more Peruvian than American, for she had lived in Peru since she was three months old. Except for brief trips to the United States with her parents, most of her life was spent in Yarinacocha. Donna had just completed two years of college and had decided to return to the translation center to work as a short-term missionary. An expert computer typist, she worked in the print shop keyboarding New Testaments in various stages of translation into indigenous languages.

As Rómulo and the others chatted with the young women, one of the teenagers mentioned that there would be a young people's meeting in a nearby town that night. "Oh, my dad is going to drive the bus," Donna offered.

"Rómulo is going to be the featured speaker," Jonatan said. "Are you going to be there to hear him speak?"

Rómulo sensed she would say yes.

"Wouldn't miss it," Donna said with a laugh.

In the days that followed, Donna and Rómulo continued crossing each other's paths. Although caught up in the translation work, Rómulo always managed to find some time to spend with her. There were many breaks and rest periods because Irma, Conrad's part-Quechua wife, was expecting their second child.

One day Irma said to Rómulo, "When you get your girlfriend in a romantic mood under an avocado tree, tell her that you'd like some avocados," she urged. Irma was craving avocados.

To Rómulo it seemed a strange way to approach Donna, especially since he disliked avocados. *But Irma has a lot more experience with these Americans,* he thought to himself. *Maybe she is on to something here.*

That evening Rómulo talked with Donna under the Jacksons' avocado tree. With all the charm he could muster, Rómulo said,

"Your beauty is as great as the taste of these avocados." Somehow the line bombed. Donna just shrugged and looked at him quizzically. At the time the large tree didn't have any ripe avocados.

The next week Donna invited Rómulo to a potluck for a small prayer group at the center. One of the most popular dishes at the supper was avocado salad. Donna offered to fill Rómulo's plate, and when she came back to their table, Rómulo groaned at the sight of a huge mound of avocado salad. "I filled your plate with it, Rómulo, because I remembered how much you like avocados."

Rómulo felt obliged to eat the salad, but he reminded himself to be more careful with compliments in the future. "That's sure great salad, Donna," he said as he finally finished the helping.

Donna immediately jumped up from the table. "I'll get you some more." Rómulo manfully waded into his second plateful of avocado salad, trying to keep a smile on his face.

In no time at all Rómulo was certain of one thing—he wanted to marry Donna. The third day after they had met, he announced to her, "I'm going to marry you."

Donna put him off. "I'm not sure I'm going to marry anyone at the moment, Rómulo," Donna said marveling at the confidence he had in their new friendship.

For the next two weeks the pair spent as much time together as they could, but there was no further talk of marriage or any other kind of commitment. Rómulo returned to Lima with the Phelpses and then headed home to Ayacucho. He promised to write to Donna, and she agreed to keep in touch.

One day Donna received a letter from Rómulo inviting her to visit him in Chakiqpampa.

"How can I do it?" Donna asked co-worker Patsy Adams. "My dad won't let me go alone. Will you go with me?"

Patsy threw her hands up. "There's no way I can go with you

on that trip," she said with a laugh. "It's not right for the two of us to do it. You should take your father along."

Art Jackson, a skilled mechanic, occasionally traveled to Ayacucho, and Donna hoped he would soon have a reason to go back.

What does Dad think about my relationship with Rómulo? Donna wondered, doubting she would ever get his approval. *Guess it doesn't matter what Dad thinks since I've not made up my own mind about Rómulo. Besides we're only good friends.*

When Rómulo returned to the mountains, Art hoped that that would be the end of the relationship. Though the Jacksons had raised their children to love Peruvian culture, they had watched many mixed marriages go through the identity crisis of living in two worlds—indigenous and American—and they were convinced that Donna would be better off marrying a North American. Art prayed for wisdom. He didn't want to turn Donna away from the family by standing against his strong-willed daughter. But like any father, he wanted her to have the best possible husband.

It was not long before a power line outage at the Wycliffe Quicapata center just outside of Ayacucho needed Art's attention. The father and daughter caught a flight to Lima. There Rómulo met them at the airport, and soon the trio was traveling by bus to Ayacucho. Shortly after they arrived, Rómulo finished arranging the last details for the trek to Chakiqpampa. Early one morning the three set off in a Land Rover. They went as far as the road would take them, to a village near Chakiqpampa called Paccha. Here they arranged for a safe place to leave the vehicle overnight, and then they began hiking the last leg of the trip.

Rómulo chattered excitedly as they walked the mountain trail, but Art and Donna began to tire from the thin air. With foresight, Rómulo had arranged for some horses to be brought to a particularly steep part of the trail. Art and Donna climbed on their mounts, but when Art went for the stirrups, much to his surprise, his feet dragged on the ground on either side. Though he didn't consider himself particularly tall, the horses were unusually small. Art could see that it would be more efficient just to walk the trail—at his own pace.

Further up the trail they crossed an ancient stone bridge. As they reached the other side, they met a procession coming down toward the cemetery. Several men were struggling under the weight of the body of a young woman lying on a stretcher. They said she had died in childbirth.

"Can you give us some money for the family and the funeral?" one of the men asked.

Never one to refuse any need he could meet, Rómulo immediately dug into his pockets and pulled out several bills, which he handed to the man. Just then a young man galloped up on a sweat-lathered horse. He shouted in a drunken rage as he edged past the group and off across the bridge. Someone said he was the dead woman's husband.

Rómulo decided it was best to move on quickly. "Let's keep going. These people know only one way to deal with death, and that is to drink and wail and mourn for days. Someday we will give them the Scriptures so they can understand what it is to have hope in the Lord." Art Jackson was impressed by Rómulo's comment.

As they arrived in Chakiqpampa, Rómulo could hardly contain his excitement. He rushed Donna around showing off the sights and sounds of his home town and introduced her to many of his friends and neighbors.

Rómulo had planned to hold two special services during the Jacksons' two-day visit. A popular speaker, Rómulo had no trouble persuading people to come out to his grandfather's church in Chakiqpampa. The people gathered from miles around.

The first evening several women shepherds visited the service. When Rómulo gave an invitation to receive Christ as Lord, the women stepped forward.

"Will you look at that!" Art Jackson marveled.

After the service the shepherds lingered to talk with Rómulo. "We know our men would also like to accept Jesus," one explained. "Would you talk to them also?"

"Can they get here early tomorrow morning?" Rómulo asked. "That's when we're leaving for the next village."

He wanted to be sure that the Jacksons were well attended to during this visit, so although he would ordinarily have accompanied the women back to their community, this time it didn't seem possible.

"We'll be here," the new believers promised.

Despite a driving rain that fell through the night, the women returned with their husbands early the following morning. At about 4 A.M. they awoke Rómulo with a sharp knock at the door. "Brother Rómulo, are you there?" they called out.

"Yes, sisters, we're here," Rómulo answered as he crawled out of bed. With Art following close behind, Rómulo led the shepherds and their husbands into a side room and began sharing the gospel with them. Finally Rómulo turned to Art and asked, "Brother Art, will you pray with us?"

Together Rómulo and Art led the men to accept Jesus Christ, an experience which would forever change Art's impression of Rómulo. *I don't know if Donna will marry Rómulo or not,* Art thought. *He loves Jesus so much and has such a heart to reach his people. I'm sure Donna could do a lot worse for a husband, but she probably won't do any better.*

After this brief visit, Donna and Art returned to the Yarinacocha translation center. Any romance would have to continue through letters—but the distance between them was about to increase.

For years Rómulo had dreamed of studying the Bible in the United States. One day he met Richard Steel, a missionary with the Assemblies of God church.

"If you'd like to study in the U.S., Rómulo, you should consider the Latin American Bible Institute in Los Angeles. The classes are taught in Spanish."

Rómulo recognized the name. It was the school where Nicky Cruz, one of his heroes, had studied. Cruz was the author of the fascinating book *Run, Baby, Run*, which had been a favorite of his and the students of the University Bible Circle in Ayacucho.

Conrad helped Rómulo open a bank account for his earnings from the translation work, and along with the other missionaries, began helping him gather the paperwork he would need to obtain a visa to study abroad.

After months of waiting for word from the U.S. Embassy, the visa finally came. Armed with his savings and other gifts, Rómulo headed off to college in January of 1977. The New Testament was nearly complete, and his help was no longer needed.

Rómulo boarded the plane with a touch of nervousness, well aware that this was not just another flight between Ayacucho and Lima. *I'm so glad Danny's going to meet me in Huntington Beach,* he thought. Danny O'Brien, a Wycliffe missionary living in California, and Rómulo had become friends when Danny lived at the Quicapata center.

The first thing Danny noticed as Rómulo came down the jetway was that he carried a very small suitcase. The order of the day would be to take Rómulo shopping. In the following days, Danny showed Rómulo around the city and helped him get settled at the college. Rómulo quickly made friends with a group of young men and embraced his studies with great fervor.

Word of a dynamic new preacher quickly spread through the Spanish-speaking congregations riddling the Los Angeles area. Rómulo's story of how Jesus had come to his mountain village of Chakiqpampa and transformed life after life—including his—fascinated them. Soon invitations to preach and share his testimony poured in.

One afternoon Rómulo called Danny O'Brien. "Danny, I've

got a problem. I need some transportation to get around to all these churches where I've been invited to preach for the Lord."

"Well, Rómulo. I'll see what I can do," Danny offered.

Danny had a friend, Ken Farson, who fixed up old cars and then gave them away to missionaries.

"Ken, you need to meet Rómulo Sauñe. He's not a missionary, but he's going to be one to his people after he gets through Bible school. What he needs is good transportation. Would you give me a call if you find a suitable car?" Danny asked.

A few days later Ken called. "I've got just the car for Rómulo, Danny. Bring him around as soon as you get a chance."

That afternoon Rómulo and Danny went over to Ken's house in Glendale. Out front was parked an eight-year-old Chevrolet sedan. "It's in good running condition," Ken said. "I know it doesn't look like much, but if you have a problem, just call me."

Rómulo thought the car was beautiful. "Look at this, Danny!" he cried out as he ran his fingers along the curves of the sedan. "Let's try it out." He flung open the door.

"Hold up, Rómulo," Danny said. "Do you have a valid driver's license?"

"Sure do," Rómulo said. He pulled out his wallet to show it.

Soon they were off down the hilly streets of Glendale with Rómulo at the wheel. They headed up a freeway ramp, and Rómulo careened into traffic cutting across the lanes and weaving around fast-moving cars. Sweat began to pour off Danny's forehead. He forced himself to say calmly, "Rómulo, you must stay between the lines."

Rómulo looked across the seat at his friend in surprise. "Oh, is that what those lines are for? We don't have them in Peru."

After a few hours of practice, Rómulo was comfortable driving American-style. And Danny agreed to let him take the car back to the Bible school.

The invitations to speak at area churches increased. Whether he spoke to adults or children, Rómulo's infectious laughter and friendliness always captivated his audience. One day a friend gave Rómulo a complete flannelgraph set about the life of Christ. Armed with this new tool, Rómulo gained in popularity in the Latino churches scattered throughout Southern California.

But beyond the scope of his children's ministry, Rómulo found another outlet for his creative talents. He and a fellow student, Juan Korzyk, were invited to help Eddie and Naomi Farrell produce Bible story tapes in Spanish for their ministry, Trans World Vision. Rómulo and Juan took turns playing different characters from the Bible, and Naomi was amazed by the creativity and energy they put into their work.

When the electronics engineer couldn't come into the studio, Rómulo and Juan phoned him up and asked for help with the technical details. Soon the two students mastered the wizardry of the recording studio, learning how to work and maintain the editing machines and professional recorders.

After Rómulo had completed the work for the Farrells, he asked for permission to begin recording the Ayacucho New Testament. He hoped it would be used for broadcasts to his people back home in Peru. The New Testament had been completed, much to his joy and satisfaction, and now he felt an urgency to get it out to his people. The thought of his mother hearing the words of Christ in her own language for the first time quickened his efforts. For Rómulo, all those years of hard work to realize the dreams he had held in his heart were beginning to pay off.

While Rómulo studied at Latin America Bible Institute, his long-distance relationship with Donna in Peru seemed to be flourishing. One summer she returned to the United States to begin linguistics training at the University of Texas in Arlington. Rómulo invited her to come out for a visit in California, and to make sure she would come, he sent her an airplane ticket.

The couple spent several wonderful days together exploring

Los Angeles and getting to know each other again. During the visit, however, Rómulo said nothing about marriage or engagement—much to Donna's surprise. As they waited for her flight back to Texas in the Los Angeles airport, Rómulo talked about how much fun they had had. Just as Donna's flight was called, Rómulo reached into his pocket and casually placed a ring on her finger.

In the excitement of catching the flight, Donna could only say good-bye, give Rómulo a quick hug, and rush onto the plane. As she sat strapped into her seat ready for takeoff, what had just transpired suddenly hit her. She thought, *Oh, no, what will Dad think? What about Mom? She's always been suspicious of Rómulo.*

When she arrived back in Texas, Donna called her parents. "Rómulo gave me a ring," she told her father.

"For your nose?" he joked. But Art Jackson gave Donna his blessing, and so did Dorothy.

In June Rómulo traveled to Dallas to visit Donna and take Greek classes with her at the Summer Institute of Linguistics. They decided to audit the class instead of taking it for credit and developed a plan to get through the intense course successfully. Rómulo's expertise was memorization, and Donna specialized in linguistic analysis. They even took the exams together, with their professor's permission, and both received an A for the course. All the time they spent together studying only increased their desire to marry soon.

Rómulo wrote his future father-in-law a lengthy letter requesting formal permission to marry Donna. The couple decided to get married in California.

Then Donna's mother called. "We've talked with our friends at Riverside Church here in Atlanta, and they would love for you to get married during their upcoming missionary conference."

"But that's Atlanta, not California," Donna protested.

"Yes, but I'm sure everyone will pitch in together to make this a wonderful wedding."

Rómulo and Donna took a hard look at their financial situation. Between the two, they had less than $50. Since the church offered to put on their reception, they accepted.

But how could they afford a wedding dress? They shopped around and finally found one for $40. It wasn't a real wedding dress, but it would serve the purpose. Sold.

Then they faced the question of how to get to Atlanta. They had no money for gasoline. So Art and Dorothy Jackson sent out a check.

Much to the couple's amazement, Riverside Church in Stone Mountain put on a beautiful wedding ceremony and reception. They provided everything down to the minutest detail, including personalized napkins and a wedding cake. A couple at the church even offered them the use of a cabin at Lookout Mountain, Tennessee, for their honeymoon before driving back to California.

At the reception many of the guests casually slipped Rómulo some money, and with these gifts the couple was able to get back to California in time for Rómulo's fall school term and to rent and outfit an apartment.

School and adjustment to marriage filled their lives for the next few months. Soon they learned that a mission that had offered to pay for Rómulo's final semester in school had not kept its promise. As graduation neared, Rómulo was unaware that the mounting school bills were not being paid. In the final week of classes, the dean of the college called him into his office.

"I've got some bad news for you, Rómulo. You can't graduate because your final semester and other expenses haven't been paid for. I'm sorry."

Stunned, Rómulo shuffled out of the office. The night before graduation, Rómulo said to Donna, "I don't want to go to the ceremonies tomorrow. Let's go to the beach instead. I don't think

I can sit there and watch all my friends graduate and not be there with them."

The two were walking hand in hand across campus when the dean's voice bellowed out from one of the administration buildings, "Rómulo, wait!" Moments later he rushed up to Rómulo with a cap and gown.

"Guess what!" he said breathlessly. "It's never happened before, but the faculty has decided to pay your outstanding bills so you can graduate. Congratulations!"

Rómulo's eyes grew wet with tears of gratitude. He could think of nothing to say except, "Praise the Lord!"

Later back at their apartment, Rómulo turned to Donna with a solemn look. "Donna, I've learned a big lesson tonight. When that mission in Santa Ana promised to pay my school fees, I grew lazy and stopped getting up at dawn to pray to the Lord. I stopped trusting in God, and I began to trust in man. Now I know that the Lord wanted me to know that He is the source of all things. We must return to praying every morning for the Lord's guidance in our lives. I never again want to take for granted God's provision."

It was a valuable lesson Rómulo and Donna Sauñe would draw on many times in the future.

7
Ayacucho for Christ

The bustling provincial city of Ayacucho perches in an otherwise quiet valley high up in the towering Andes—a rugged territory populated by the Quechua people. Before terrorism took hold of this once-calm and picturesque city, tourists wandered its cobblestone streets where hawkers sold their beautiful carvings from Piedra de Huamanga (a soapstone). In the commercial nerve center of this Spanish colonial city—the crossroads of the mountain communities—residents gathered to conduct their official business.

Through the centuries Ayacucho had also seen bloody Indian wars and the historic battles between the liberators and the Spanish conquerors. Just twenty miles away on a high plateau extending out from the foothills of the mountains, pre-Inca tribes fought violent wars where hundreds of thousands of warriors were massacred. Later, on this desolate plateau, South American liberators defeated the Spanish conquerors in the infamous Battle of Ayacucho.

The wind sweeps across the plain with great gusts of fury, and cumulus clouds blow across the sky with the speed and sound of a herd of wild horses. It is a place where the spirits of the dead still haunt those who would come near for a glimpse of the past. To some it seemed that Ayacucho would never outgrow its name, the Quechua word for "Empire" or "Corner of the Dead."

But none of that was in Rómulo's mind as he and the other members of his clan gathered for their trip to Chakiqpampa. Earlier in the day when Rómulo and Arcangel were shopping in the Ayacucho market, Rómulo had met a group of young people from the local Presbyterian church.

"You should come with us," he invited. "We are going to celebrate the goodness of the Lord for His faithfulness to His servants, like my grandfather Justiniano." They knew about the old patriarch. Who didn't?

Arcangel sidled over to Rómulo and whispered, "Nephew, can I talk to you privately?"

"Sure. Let's go over there." Rómulo pointed to a quiet corner. "What's wrong, Uncle?"

"Rómulo, are you out of your mind? Why invite a bunch of young people we barely know? I'm trying to be patient with you because you've been away for some time, and you haven't seen what it's like here in Ayacucho. You need to be more cautious. You know, the eyes and ears of the Shining Path are everywhere. These people may be a part of the Shining Path, for all we know."

"Oh, Arca, you worry too much," Rómulo said. "God is in control of our lives. One day Ayacucho will be for Christ, and we won't have to worry about such matters as the Shining Path."

"But in the meantime, try to be a little more cautious. We've got a pickup already loaded with fifteen people and all their things!"

Ayacucho always seemed to be in flux. But life had never changed more rapidly than in the late 1970s. Rómulo remembered that when he had returned to Peru from the United States in 1978, he had found Ayacucho in turmoil. It had become a hotbed of revolutionary Communist thought. The intellectuals at the University of Huamanga were well on their way to organizing one of the most ruthless revolutionary groups ever known in Latin America. Ayacucho was the birthplace of the Shining Path.

In the back of a university auditorium, Rómulo and Arcangel sat listening to Abimael Guzman. The professor of philosophy had a large following. For years he had studied the teachings of Chairman Mao Zedong. His intense desire to learn more about Mao led him to make two secret trips to China to study their economic system, government organization, and the control of their people.

The illegitimate son of a prosperous import wholesaler, Guzman eventually settled in Ayacucho, bringing with him the teachings of Mao. Even as a schoolboy at the exclusive Jesuit-run La Salle College, Guzman showed a talent for organizing students into study groups and committees.

During the early 1960s, Guzman took a professorial position at the University of San Cristobal de Huamanga. The brilliant young professor with dark-rimmed glasses and a priestly dignity began laying out his program in meticulous detail for the Shining Path. His disciples would take that path to victory, overthrow the government and set up a utopian society ruled by Guzman and his deputies. Students and sympathetic professors soon became his followers. And as their ideology evolved, it became clear that Guzman would settle for nothing less than ideological "purity."

Guzman's students called him Dr. Puka Inti, which means "Red Sun" in the Quechua language. He would often say to his disciples, "You either use power, or others will use it against you." And with a stern, professorial tone he would tell them, "I have no friends—only comrades."

Rómulo and Arcangel had frequent contact with the disciples of the Shining Path. Everyone knew about them, but at least then it was only talk. No one imagined the terror that would come later. All they knew was that if one opposed the Marxists, one would soon find himself or herself expelled from or severely criticized within the university system.

As the coordinator of the compulsory first-year requirements, Guzman taught Darwinism in such a way that it nullified any religious beliefs his mostly Roman Catholic students may have held.

With the Sino-Soviet split in 1963, Guzman's group forced the pro-Moscow Peruvian Communist Party to divide along pro-Soviet and pro-Chinese lines. And with every passing day, Guzman gained more and more extracurricular power and control at the university.

Many people in Peru believe the Shining Path is the best-organized part of society. When Shining Path followers eventually ended up in Lima prisons, they demanded to be set apart from the prison population. They maintained a rigorous discipline that surprised even the most jaded prison warden. But the Shining Path evolved into a ruthless enforcer of its own form of justice. Criminals, homosexuals, and independent thinkers were judged harshly. Those deemed unrepentant or unsuitable to society were brutally cut down.

By the late 1980s and early 1990s, Guzman's followers still believed that he held the key to resolving Peru's troubles and eagerly helped him provoke a Maoist Armageddon. In the early stages of this unprecedented revolution, Guzman's students dubbed him "Shampoo," because they said once he washed your brain, everything became crystal clear. Guzman had remarkable debating powers. Though he would have preferred the intellectual approach—persuading the indigenous and poverty-stricken masses to capture his vision for a new world, Guzman knew he would be an old man before his utopian dream became a reality that way. There had to be another way, a way to persuade the people to follow first and understand later.

Guzman understood the persuasive power of fear. As a young professor, he had set out to win the heart of Augusta de la Torre, then sixteen and the daughter of a local Communist Party chief. Although ten years her elder, Guzman stationed himself outside her house and stared at her whenever she came in or went out. At first the bizarre suitor terrified the girl, but eventually the combination of persistence and effrontery won her attention and devotion. The couple married in 1964.

The first violence came in 1969. A law restricting free high school education provoked riots in the nearby city of Huanta. Fourteen people were killed, and Guzman was temporarily jailed for inciting demonstrations against the police.

In 1970 the Shining Path came into existence as an entity in and of itself. Party members were required to memorize every word of Guzman's political writings. By 1990 cell blocks filled up with captured Shining Path fighters who labored like medieval monks, endlessly transcribing Guzman's dull speeches into notebooks. They also learned and practiced chanting the Maoist anthem, "The East Is Red," *in Chinese*—syllable by syllable.

Father Herbert Lanssiers, a Belgian-born priest who visited the Shining Path prisoners, once told a newsman, "It is a kind of engineering of the soul. Guzman created a collection of brains, like insects. It becomes a kind of mathematics from which the human factor is expelled because it brings too many impurities. The individual becomes an instrument and nothing more."

The *Sendero Luminoso* or Shining Path was devoted to the most orthodox form of Marxist-Leninism. Anxious to see his utopian world become a reality in his time, Guzman began inciting people to violence and rebellion. Beginning in 1980, Ayacucho became the center of the revolution, student disciples carrying Guzman's utopian dream into the mountain communities and beyond. They formed a network of frontline organizations that offered a sense of community to the workers, the peasants, and the women.

Cell groups led by Guzman's disciples multiplied throughout the 1970s and 1980s, forming an intricate network of highly motivated young people who believed they had no future other than this one. As the movement matured, its leaders came to the conclusion that the only way to overthrow the state was to gear up for a militant and violent assault on the Peruvian government and all that it stood for. The assault began in Ayacucho.

In 1978 Rómulo and Donna returned to Ayacucho full of dreams of turning the Corner of the Dead into part of the Kingdom of God. Ayacucho for Christ! Rómulo and his colleagues proclaimed these words wherever they went. But it was more than just a phrase. It was a declaration and a prayer that one day the people of this city and this province would bow to the God of the universe.

In 1979 two Puerto Rican evangelists arrived in Peru with plans to stage a week-long crusade in the Ayacucho municipal stadium. Rómulo had high hopes for its success, and he told the evangelists so when he guided them to the Quicapata compound guest house. Some people said the guest house was haunted or demon-possessed. But Rómulo was confident that the evangelists could handle it, although he was certain the rumors weren't true.

That night the evangelists tossed and turned in their beds. In their semi-sleepless state, voices whispered in their ears, "Your colleague is lying to you." "You are a failure." "Your wife is cheating on you." And the night was full of the sound of creaks and groans that kept them from settling into a deep sleep.

At first light the evangelists rushed to Rómulo's house and pleaded with him to find another place for them to stay. "The house is truly haunted, Rómulo," they insisted.

Rómulo was acutely discouraged. If anyone should have been able to handle the situation, it was these men of God. But they had no courage. Who would stand up to Satan in this Corner of the Dead?

That afternoon people streamed into the stadium anxious to

hear what these Puerto Ricans had to say. Rómulo stood on the podium, scanning the restless audience with concern. Instead of listening, the people insulted the evangelists, and some even threw rocks at them. By the second day, the crowd had settled down, and the evangelists were able to carry on without further incident.

By the third day, Rómulo began to relax. Things seemed to be going well. At the end of the service, the evangelists called forward all those who wanted to receive a healing from God. Many pressed forward, some in wheelchairs, others carried by their friends.

Suddenly Rómulo saw a storm gathering in the distance. The idyllic spring day was about to come under siege. Boiling black clouds rolled in incredibly fast. And then there was a tremendous clap of thunder, and bolts of lightning shot out with a force that electrified the air above the stadium. A fearful silence descended over the crowd. Then with another explosion, the clouds burst and a torrential rain fell on the stadium. The crowd scattered in a chaos of overturned wheelchairs as they raced for cover. But there was precious little of it, and people cowered along the outside walls, unsure of where to run to next.

Margarita Fajardo had volunteered to usher at the crusade. Each day she had encouraged her husband Alfredo to attend the services—but he declined. "Margarita, I'm not interested," he would say over and over again. But Margarita insisted. And finally she devised a way to get Alfredo to at least some of the services.

"Would you be willing to shuttle the evangelists back and forth from the stadium to the Quicapata center?" she had asked hopefully. To please her, he agreed. Each day Margarita would pray for her husband's salvation. Though he often found a reason to leave the stadium, sometimes he came back early enough to hear the last few minutes of the sermon. Margarita hoped the seeds being planted in his heart would take root.

When the cloud burst over the stadium, Margarita looked for Alfredo. He had not yet arrived. A woman who had come forward for prayer now grabbed at her and screamed, "Save me! Save me! How do you pray? It's the end of the world, and I've got to know!" Margarita wrenched free. It was too late for her to deal with the woman, for the sky turned into a swirling, boiling ocean, unloading an apocalyptic shower of hail the size of pheasant eggs. The Quechuas called such a phenomenon *maruntupar,* or the rain of eggs. Soon the stadium was covered in a white blanket of ice.

At the first hint of trouble, Rómulo had rushed off the stage, and now Margarita saw him running back and forth carrying the lame to safety. The hail fell so hard that people cried out in pain.

Margarita noticed a small sheltered section of the stadium and ran to it, but suddenly she stopped in horror. "Where is Pachin?" Her two-year-old son had been left with some friends, and now she couldn't see them. "Pachin! Pachin!" she screamed.

An older man came running out to her. "Don't worry, Margarita. The brethren have taken your son to the players' changing room. He's fine."

As chaos reigned in the stadium, Donna grabbed her son Rumi and crawled under the podium. The hail fell so thickly that when it ended some time later, they were trapped until someone heard their cries and came to the rescue.

Hours later after Rómulo had brought the evangelists safely home, he sat with Donna in discouragement. "When will Ayacucho be for Christ?" he asked sadly. "My back is hurting."

"Here, let's take a look." Donna helped him remove his shirt. His back was a mass of purple and blue bruises. "Oh, Rómulo, did this happen when you helped the people find shelter in the storm?" He nodded weakly.

A few days after the crusade, Rómulo and Donna dropped by a popular coffee shop in downtown Ayacucho. The talk was of the crusade and all that had happened.

"What about that hail, Rómulo?" one man ventured. "Was it from God or from Satan?"

"That's an interesting question," Rómulo said noncommittally. "What do you think?"

"I'm sure God was punishing the Protestants for having such a crusade," one man blurted out.

"God wasn't punishing us," another man piped up. "He was demonstrating His great power and might."

"Some power and might. The crusade was over when that hail started falling," said a woman from the corner table. "I think it was Satan trying to destroy the crusade and keep people from joining the Protestants."

The debate disheartened Rómulo. It seemed he would never hear the last of it, and he had no ready explanation for what had happened.

Seven years later in 1986, Rómulo agreed to help organize another crusade. Two evangelists from El Salvador were invited to speak and hold healing services in the mile-high city. Rómulo would act as host and Quechua translator.

Just the thought of hundreds of people attending the crusade and hearing of the love of God filled Rómulo with excitement. But from past experience he knew to curb his joy. Instead he tried to prepare himself for whatever might happen to jeopardize the crusade.

When the evangelists arrived, Rómulo showed them to their quarters in his parents' home. The high altitude and thin air quickly wore them out, and they settled in for a nap. Ayacucho is located some 9,000 feet above sea level, and it usually takes a few days for visitors to adjust.

After they fell asleep, one of the evangelists was awakened by whispers in his ears, "Curse your partner." "Curse him . . . curse him . . . curse him . . ."

The evangelist was petrified. In all his years of preaching in Central America and beyond, he had never experienced anything like this. "In the name of the Lord Jesus Christ, leave me alone. You have no power over me through the spotless blood of the Lamb that was slain!" he commanded.

As suddenly as they had come, the whispers ceased. The room was still. The evangelist shook his partner awake and told him what had happened. "That's strange," he said sleepily. "I was just dreaming the same thing."

The two went out to find Rómulo, and together they prayed that God would put his hand over them and give them peace. And they asked the Lord to dispel the forces of darkness that had such a stronghold in Ayacucho.

That night Rómulo climbed out of bed at about 1 A.M. and headed toward the bathroom. As he walked past the two evangelists sleeping in the next room, he paused to offer a prayer for them. "Lord, You know these brothers have come a long distance to proclaim Your Word here in Ayacucho. Give them a deep sense of Your presence and a peace that passes all understanding. Thank You for the rest that You are giving them tonight."

A moment later he returned to his bedroom still thinking about what lay ahead in this wonderful week of meetings. Suddenly his bedroom door swung open with a loud PHWAA! An enormous dark figure filled the doorway. Its eyes glowed red, and its teeth were black and rotting.

"Hah, hah, hah!" the figure laughed spitefully. "You're happy," it hissed, "because you've brought two evangelists from El Salvador. But this will count for nothing. I've called up my demons from Nicaragua to help us fight you here in Ayacucho."

With another burst of evil laughter, the demon continued, "You don't have any power in this city. It's our territory. You know it in your heart and spirit. And as for your crusade . . . you might as well cancel it. It won't make any difference." Hideous laughter rang in Rómulo's ears.

Scripture, Rómulo thought as he felt his fear nearing hysteria. He wracked his mind for some Bible verses. Nothing came to him. He was transfixed by the glowing red eyes. He groped around his bed stand for his Bible. He always kept one somewhere near his bed. Where was it? Finally his fingers brushed against it, and he grabbed it. With God's truth firmly in his hands, his fear evaporated, and he held it up toward the spirit. "You have no power over us," he declared. "In the name of Jesus and by the spotless blood of the Lamb of God, be gone. You've already been defeated by the blood of Jesus Christ."

The figure suddenly vanished in the darkness. Only then did Rómulo realize that his sheets were soaked with sweat, and he was trembling with fear. The rest of the night he tossed and turned, but sleep never came.

The next morning Rómulo recounted what had happened to the astonished evangelists. "We've been talking," one of the evangelists said. "At different times both of us felt the same spirit in our rooms." The men joined together in prayer for the crusade, asking that God's power would reach into the hearts of the people of Ayacucho. "Ayacucho for Christ!" they proclaimed in faith at the end of their prayers.

In a quiet moment of that day, Rómulo reflected on his encounter with the demon. *The demon had said that he was sending for reinforcements from Nicaragua.* At that time in Nicaragua the Contra war against the Sandinista regime was bringing terrible bloodshed and senseless loss of life. "This same spirit of violence lives in our mountains. The violent spirits from Nicaragua. Oh, Lord," he prayed, "guide us through these difficult times and give us strength to proclaim Your Word."

That week the crusade went forward as planned, and there were no further incidents.

During the 1960s, the problems and pressures of Peruvian society had begun to seep into the remote Quechua hamlets and villages. Contact between the two cultures had increased with the advent of modern communication and transportation. The Quechuas were reaching out beyond their world, just as certain sectors of the Peruvian *mestizo* culture were expanding up into the Andean highlands. Life was in flux for both cultures.

Justiniano and Fernando Quicaña anxiously viewed the inroads being made by Peru's Communist Party. Cadres were visiting the isolated Quechua communities and indoctrinating the leaders with a completely foreign ideology. Justiniano had heard about nearby communities where Quechuas had revolted against their wealthy landowners and claimed their "rights."

Such upheaval disturbed him. He did not want to see his community rebel against the Catholic nuns who held title to their land. Something had to be done quickly, or their fields would be turned into "cooperative farms," which to him meant loss of control over how he chose to manage his land. The Catholic nuns had never placed any significant demands on Chakiqpampa, and they had lived in relative peace.

One evening as Justiniano talked it over with Fernando and other leaders of the community, he devised a clever plan to defuse any notions of revolt.

"We will buy the land from the nuns," he announced. "Each family will contribute whatever it can, and we will pool all of our resources to offer the nuns a fair price." Fernando was chosen as the accountant because he was the best-educated. He helped his neighbors calculate the value of a pig or a bushel of grain, and all these things were entered into a ledger. Soon they had gathered together enough to make an offer.

The purchase went through uneventfully, and the community held a great celebration. The Communists would gain no foothold in Chakiqpampa, for the people already owned the land.

But the peace would not last long. By the 1970s, Ayacucho was embroiled in a new ideological war, one that would eventually pit brother against brother and community against community. The upheaval would tear apart families and turn thriving villages into wasteland. The people would flee to the unfamiliar cities of the Spanish where they would be exploited and stripped of their dignity. Still that would be a small price to pay to escape the terror that had driven them to near insanity.

Inspired by Abimael Guzman, Ayacucho's students began fanning out into the highlands spreading their ideas for a new world. For Justiniano, there was only one message for the world, the message of salvation through Jesus Christ. This would lead him on a collision course that would demand the ultimate sacrifice. Had he known this, he probably would have changed nothing. Such was the strength of his convictions that to move in any direction other than toward the Savior was to go backward. For centuries his people had been locked in the darkness of their fears. Jesus had come to bring light and give them hope for the future. For Justiniano, that was the only message worth proclaiming.

The Quicaña home was known as a haven for weary travelers. Here one could be sure of receiving a hot meal and place to rest in peace. Also a traveler could expect to hear the Word preached. No one left the household without a word of encouragement from the Scriptures. But as the intellectuals of the University of Huamanga began to spread their influence throughout Ayacucho, the welcome mat outside Justiniano and Teofila's home became a source of growing irritation. Too many young people were influenced by the patriarch's gospel. The literature that Justiniano gave his visitors as they went on their way led people away from the ideology that would soon come to be known around the world as the Shining Path.

In the 1980s the intellectuals took up arms and launched a wave of terror and violence in an effort to force a radical revolution. The country seemed headed into chaos. As visitors dropped by the Quicaña home, the talk often turned toward the young revolutionaries. Some travelers leaned toward the goals of the

Shining Path. For too long poverty had reigned in their communities. It was time for change, and only violent revolution could bring it, they repeated to Justiniano. But others leaned toward the military. It was more important to have order. No one had ever cared about their backward communities. Why should they believe an ideology so foreign to their culture?

Justiniano and Teofila listened patiently, avoiding any attempts to draw them into either party. Rather they would steer the conversation away from politics and to the hope of the cross. Only faith in Jesus would bring true peace. Many listened. But others came away from Chakiqpampa with hearts hardened against the old couple who refused to accept the new ways.

When the indoctrinated youth would hike down from the mountains with their rifles and bark orders at the village leaders, Justiniano rarely listened to them. Instead he would chastise them for the violence they used to subjugate entire communities.

The violence had driven the missionaries out, and the Quechua Christians felt isolated. The revolution was in full force. In this time of uncertainty, the church became an indirect victim of the war. If one were to offer a cup of water to a terrorist, the army would retaliate. And vice versa. There seemed to be no way to survive. Yet through it all a comforting beacon of light and hope emanated from the humble Quicaña home in Chakiqpampa.

For a time Justiniano's witness was tolerated because of his position of authority in the community. In many ways he was untouchable, and no one wanted to silence this great voice.

One day in 1984 a rumor streaked through the village that the *Senderistas* or Shining Path revolutionaries were planning to attack Chakiqpampa. Justiniano packed a small bag and fled for the safety of a neighboring town. He knew he was a target, and it was best to be cautious. Teofila, his wife, stayed behind to watch over their property. "You're an old woman," he told her. "No one will bother you."

At the appointed hour, a squad of government soldiers entered the village. Some assumed they were in pursuit of the revolutionaries. The nervous soldiers began to search door to door, dragging out would-be rebel collaborators, anyone who had information as to the whereabouts of the terrorists. Before long they were banging on Teofila's door.

"We've heard that you've been feeding and housing members of the Shining Path," the squad commander accused. "That's against Peruvian law. I charge you with criminal behavior."

"It's our custom, young man, to feed anyone who comes asking for help," Teofila explained. "Ever since I was a young woman when my husband and I built this house, we've always welcomed travelers through our town. It's our way. Now I'm just an old woman. Leave me alone!"

"We're mounting an investigation for the military about your subversive activities," the uniformed officer said.

"Go away and come back when you're sober. We're not subversives. We just feed travelers; we don't ask about their politics," Teofila explained.

The man began making notes on a note pad. "You admit to entertaining strangers—probably members of the Shining Path. Maybe they are your comrades," he sneered. "We know they use old women like you as their spies and informants. What a perfect cover. I arrest you for withholding information."

Then he slapped Teofila.

"Where is your husband? Where are your sons?" he demanded. When Teofila refused to answer, the officer nodded to his subordinates who began to torch the Quicaña house. Quickly flames engulfed the simple frame house. Teofila wiped the tears from her eyes, refusing to give up an inch of her dignity.

"Where is your husband?" the officer asked once more.

"Justiniano is in Ayacucho on a trip, and my sons are in Huancayo," she answered with a slight tremor. "It's the truth."

The officer slapped Teofila again and told her to shut up. With a motion to his lieutenant, two soldiers grabbed her and shoved her toward the trail leading out of the village. Teofila stumbled but managed to maintain her balance. Her heart ached as the family home and all their belongings were being destroyed—the memories of happiness there going up in thick, black smoke. She wept as she was pushed and shoved down the mountain trail.

The soldiers finally led her to where they had parked their truck. Teofila was tossed into the back, and they drove off to their encampment many miles away from Chakiqpampa.

For days the soldiers tortured the elderly grandmother. First they threw her into a pool of water. Then they forced her to stand on top of a rocky ledge for an entire day. Then it was back to the frigid pool. Each time the officer in charge prodded her with questions, the interrogations becoming harsher with each punishment. Finally after fifteen days, the commander gathered his men around.

"From my perspective, sometimes old women are best," he said with a knowing smile. The others laughed as they caught their commander's meaning. Then in a final act of humiliation, they each took a turn raping her. There was nothing more to be done with this woman. If she had any information, she would die with it. As evening drew near, they loaded her onto a truck and drove her to a remote field where they dumped her naked body. No one doubted that the old woman was dead. Then they drove off in the darkness.

The bitter cold that often sets in at the highest elevations of the Andean mountains chilled Teofila Quicaña's abused body. But mercifully she lay unconscious on a thick bed of tundra grass. As the sun slowly rose the next morning over the mountain peaks and fingers of light spread out across the treeless meadows, Teofila's frigid body began to respond to the warmth. Despite the lacerations and bruises that caused her to cry out in pain, she forced herself to begin walking. Mile after mile she walked until she reached a small clearing where she collapsed in the arms of the startled peasant who responded to her faint knock on the door.

Although the Quicañas were well known in the region, no one recognized her as Teofila. Soon word was sent out that a woman had been found. The Quicaña family members who had been frantically searching for their matriarch came to her place of shelter. Upon entering the darkly lit room, they hardly recognized her.

Teofila was taken to Ayacucho to the intensive care ward of the hospital. There with the help of her family and her strong faith, she soon recovered completely.

The community helped Justiniano and Teofila rebuild their home in Chakiqpampa. And in time life returned to normal. God had preserved their lives and given them more days to bring glory to His name.

Rómulo's eternal optimism tended to carry him forward through whatever circumstances came his way. In 1982 the Bible society notified him that the New Testament he had worked on was ready to be dedicated. After years of work with words and paper and books, Rómulo rejoiced to hold the precious Word of God in his hands. This time it was in his own language, the language of the Quechuas of Ayacucho. More than a black book with binding and paper, it was God's Word for His people in a language they could clearly understand. "Father, thank You," Rómulo prayed. "Help us as we distribute this book to the people. May they read it and apply it to their lives."

Al Shannon, the lanky missionary with Wycliffe Bible Translators who had been a long-time friend of the Quicaña-Sauñe clan, met with Rómulo, Fernando Quicaña, and the other Quechua church leaders to help plan the dedication of the New Testament.

Finally the day arrived. It was a beautiful Sunday in January 1982. Rómulo had planned a day-long celebration, beginning with a morning worship service for which he asked Homer Emerson, the first Bible translator to Peru, to preach the message.

Wycliffe missionary Al Shannon would preach in the afternoon. As that service came to an end, the missionary translators who had worked on the Ayacucho New Testament paired up with all the Quechua co-translators and presented each with a copy of the completed New Testament. Then the Bible society opened up a booth, and the New Testaments went on sale for everyone.

As the stacks of New Testaments rapidly flowed off the tables into the eager hands of the Quechua believers, no one was more surprised than the head of the Peruvian Bible Society. All the New Testaments were sold out in minutes, and still the people clamored for more.

During the weeks that followed, an additional 5,000 copies of the New Testament were sold or distributed. And it happened none too soon, for less than a month later the government imposed martial law, and all the missionaries abandoned the region leaving the church to fend for itself. Yet even in the rising tide of terrorism sweeping the land, still another 5,000 New Testaments got into the hands of Quechua believers.

The following five years were extremely difficult ones in Ayacucho. The violence had increased, but providentially God had allowed the New Testament to get into the churches just before the terrorism took hold in the mountain communities. Knowing that the people had God's Word comforted Rómulo and the other Quechua church leaders. The believers would need to draw on God's strength to endure the many trials ahead.

Many of Ayacucho's young people were heeding the call to overthrow the government through violent revolution. Unlike his grandfather, Rómulo never spoke out against the fighters, nor did he allow any member of his family to make public remarks that would alienate them from the revolutionaries. Rómulo loved many of them, for he had known them during his high school years. Often one would allow Rómulo to pray with him, and he even led some to the Lord.

One day in the streets of Ayacucho, Rómulo saw one of his childhood friends, Juan. "It's been a long time since we've seen each other," Rómulo said. "Let's get a soda at this cafe and catch up."

Juan agreed and the pair sat down to talk. After reminiscing about their school days, Juan said, "The teachings of Professor Guzman make a lot of sense to me. I've joined the Shining Path. They've even trained me to shoot their weapons. What about you, Rómulo? Are you still questioning our cause?"

"Tell me more about the weapons," Rómulo prompted his friend. "Have you used these guns on anyone?"

At that, Juan stared at the floor, and Rómulo could sense his sadness. "Yes, Rómulo. I've used those weapons. The other night we came into one of the communities, and my leader insisted that we kill even the women and children. It has been tearing at my heart ever since."

Rómulo looked at him with compassion. "Only Jesus has the power to forgive you for this violence. What you need is the love of Christ to fill your life." Then Rómulo led his friend to the truth of God's Word and how He could give him a new life in Christ.

"Can I do this now?" Juan asked.

"Yes, you can pray after me," Rómulo encouraged.

They prayed together. When Juan looked up, the fear and sadness had evaporated from his eyes, and he was at peace with himself.

"Here, I want to give you this to help you in your faith," said Rómulo handing Juan a Quechua New Testament. Then he put his arms around his friend and prayed for him again. Juan was one of several young rebels Rómulo led out of the Shining Path and into the welcoming arms of Jesus.

8

More Than a Dirge

There had been so many delays that Rómulo thought his party would never get on their way to Chakiqpampa. But finally by noon they were ready to leave. Those who were to ride in Arcangel's white pickup hopped aboard—Rómulo in front with his parents, his brother Ruben, his friend Margarita and her daughter Keila, and Arcangel at the wheel. In the back were a number of friends and relatives.

Arcangel had the radio playing softly. Rómulo recognized the Andean music with pan flutes carrying a mournful tune. It brought to the surface once-buried memories of his childhood. In his mind's eye he could see a little shepherd boy playing his flute as he watched his flock of sheep grazing on the hillsides. Now wherever he traveled he carried along his *quena,* and often he would play a tune for his foreign friends to give them just a taste of the culture of the mountains—Quechua music. And Rómulo's love for music had helped revolutionize worship in the Quechua church.

By 1978 the Quechua church had developed a mature leadership. There were thousands of Quechua believers throughout the vast Andean mountains, living in isolated communities or in the marginal neighborhoods of larger cities and villages.

Anthropologist Tito Paredes had a keen interest in the Peruvian indigenous church. As an evangelical Christian, he understood better than most the need for the Quechua church to develop its own expression of faith and spiritual identity. Its adaptation of Western culture had hampered rather than encouraged spiritual worship. Something had to be done.

Paredes's theological training and his interest in Peru's native cultures gave him an idea. In 1978 he talked to Quechua leaders about gathering native leaders, from as many denominations as would come, to form a committee.

Some thirty-one leaders representing five denominations and three parachurch organizations agreed to come. Perhaps there would be a way to bring back a sense of unity, they hoped. Fernando Quicaña was the most hopeful. An intellectually oriented leader of men, the thoughtful Fernando had dreamed of a moment such as this. Eagerly he joined his fellow Quechua believers in the meeting hall and listened as Tito Paredes began the session.

Standing before the men—all leaders in their own right— Paredes began to talk about unity in the Quechua church. He spoke, he listened, he proposed, and he held up work models he believed would lead to more dialogue and cooperation between the denominations.

It was an exciting moment. Fernando's heart soared. "Finally," he breathed, "our day has come. We don't have to be divided by the gospel. We can be unified in the Lord, regardless of our denomination."

Paredes could tell that Fernando was anxious to speak. "Please, Brother Fernando," he encouraged, "share with us what you believe is the solution to the issues that divide your people."

Fernando eagerly stepped forward. He gazed out across the room and smiled, his keen brown eyes sparkling. "For years we have accepted the wisdom of the missionaries and the Spanish leadership of the Peruvian church. We have sung their hymns, we have learned to play their instruments, we have organized our churches as they instructed us, and we have tried to honor God through it all.

"But I think you will all agree with me that we have not sensed that our faith is truly ours," he continued. "I believe it is time that we begin to express our faith in our own way, with our own music, with our own instruments, and within the context of our own culture."

Several Quechua men sang out, "Amen, brother," but most of the audience remained silent. What Fernando was proposing was too radical for some.

"Brothers," Fernando concluded, "what we need is something truly ours, something that will revive our sense of *ayllu* and bring us all back together."

After hours of dialogue, the leaders agreed to form an association that would guide their move toward a Quechua interpretation of the gospel. With Paredes's skillful organizing abilities, the group set down the bylaws. It was a moment of great joy, and the men raised their voices in praise to the Lord and thanksgiving for the renewed pride they felt in being Quechua.

Fernando and others in Ayacucho believed that in the context of *ayllu,* or community support, the gospel of Jesus Christ could make significant inroads. But could they help the isolated communities understand that the gospel was fully theirs, in the context of their own culture—not something that belonged to foreigners or to the Latin church?

Through the years they had faithfully preached the gospel in their churches—Presbyterian, Pentecostal, Seventh-Day Adventist, and many others. Yet few denominational leaders were open to doing things the Quechua way. Was it true that the accordion was the only musical instrument that had a place in the church? Nothing could be more foreign to the Quechua believer.

One missionary once told Enrique, Rómulo's father, to destroy his guitar. "That's the instrument of the devil," he said. "Get rid of that thing." So Enrique, a new believer in the faith who wanted to submit to leadership, destroyed his beautiful guitar. And many other brethren in the Quechua church did likewise.

Though they tried to learn the unfamiliar rhythms and melodies of the music taught by the missionaries and the national church, little of it found a place in the heart of the Andean people.

One afternoon as Fernando and Arcangel sat outside Grandfather Justiniano Quicaña's house in Chakiqpampa, their conversation turned to the problems facing the Quechua church. The last decade had brought so many changes into the Quechua communities. The future seemed uncertain. The economic woes that plagued Peru were compounded in the countryside. Farmers were barely making a living. They had little hope for change.

"Why have we Christians allowed ourselves to become so separated from our communities, Fernando?" Arcangel asked. "Why is it that our people suffer so? There's so much we could do for them if believers were willing to work together."

"Yes," Fernando agreed sadly. "Before the gospel came to our people, we used to always get together for festivals; we would work together on community projects; we helped each other in the spirit of *ayllu*."

"But we get together for church activities," Arcangel noted. "Hasn't the good news about Jesus joined us together in unity?"

Fernando smiled at his younger brother. "We shouldn't be too discouraged, little brother. One day we will bring our communities together again, but with the power of the gospel in the context of our culture. We need to bring hope to our people; we need to help bring them out of their backwardness.

"But we'll never do it if we can't overcome petty denominational differences," Fernando said. "The Presbyterians won't meet with the Pentecostals, and the Seventh-Day Adventists don't want to meet with anyone. And no one is interested in working with the Catholics. What we need is to bring everyone together, but we must do it in the Quechua way, Arcangel."

Over the next few months the Quechua Evangelical Committee led by Fernando and several others met on an irregular basis. But some felt inhibited by the oversight they sensed from the Spanish churches. What they really wanted was something they could call their own, completely independent of the Latin culture, solely Quechua.

At a gathering of Quechua church leaders, Fernando laid out his vision. It was agreed that the Quechua Evangelical Committee should eventually develop into an independent mission. The mission would be led entirely by Quechua leaders and focus exclusively on meeting the spiritual, material, and physical needs of the Quechua nation. It eventually came to be known as Tawantinsuyuman Allin Willakuy Apaqkuna or TAWA. It meant, "Taking the Good News to the four corners of the Quechua world," an adaptation of the old Inca *Tawantinsuyu*, or the four corners of the earth over which the Incas had ruled.

This same year, 1978, Rómulo and Donna returned to Ayacucho. It was an uncertain time. The university students who had once been contented to sit through hours of lectures by Abimael Guzman and his followers were ready for action. It was time to put the lessons into practice. Political flyers flowed out of the University of Huamanga. The streets were littered with their political placards and leaflets.

Fernando immediately briefed Rómulo on what was happening. "Rómulo, what we want to do is find a way to pacify the antagonism between the different denominations and form a bond based on Scripture."

"Uncle," Rómulo exclaimed, "that's wonderful. You know I've come back specifically because I want to serve my people in whatever way I can."

Though the mission was just beginning to get on its feet, Rómulo jumped in full of enthusiasm and ideas. In the little

Quechua church of La Libertad, several of the young men had begun writing Christian words for popular Quechua tunes and performing these new songs at services. One afternoon Rómulo dropped by the church during a practice session. Unlike the traditional piano or accordion music and translated songs from the Spanish culture, the music was wonderfully familiar with the rhythm and pentatonic melodies of his childhood.

When the young men saw Rómulo slip into the room, they quickly lowered their instruments. The leader, Walter Parado, smiled and tried to explain. "Rómulo, we're singing Quechua Christian songs we've written ourselves."

Rómulo rushed to the front. "Brothers! This is wonderful. Please don't stop playing. This is just the reason why I've come back to work with you. Our music is beautiful, and we should use it to praise God."

Motioning them to continue, Rómulo sat down and hummed along since he didn't yet know the words. Tears welled up in his eyes as he thought of the potential such music had to unlock the gospel for his people.

When he heard of Rómulo's response, Fernando was overjoyed. "I thought you would forget about your culture when you went to the States," he told him. "But I can see that you are truly with us now."

What Fernando didn't know was that tucked away in Rómulo's bag throughout his years of travel overseas was the little shepherd's flute. Once as Rómulo had played a tune within earshot of a church old-timer, the man had scolded, "That's the music of the drunks. Rómulo, you're a believer in Jesus Christ now. Throw away that flute!"

Discouraged, Rómulo had put the flute away, but he couldn't part with his dreams. One day there would be a way to bring Quechua music into the church to the glory of God.

As Rómulo settled back into life in Ayacucho, his enthusiasm for the newly emerging Quechua-style gospel music took a new turn. One day he visited with a group of musicians who were learning some of the new songs he had written. After the encouraging practice session, they eagerly gathered around Rómulo.

"Rómulo, those songs are beautiful," one of the young men complimented him.

Another added, "Do you think we could play these for the church sometime?"

Rómulo nodded. "I've been thinking for some time now that we should form a group to travel around sharing this music with our people. It will be a wonderful way to introduce the gospel to them, don't you think?"

They all agreed. "Let's name our group The Messengers of God."

But they knew the churches would resist their style of worship. Rómulo encouraged them, "Brothers, let's not worry about what others will say. If we remember to always give God the glory, He will make their hearts receptive to our music."

Samuel Saccsara, the guitar player, could hardly believe what he was hearing. A slightly built young man in his early twenties, he had spent his teenage years playing in musical groups around the city but had never felt entirely fulfilled. What he wanted was to compose and play Quechua music in the church. Until Rómulo came on the scene, he had never quite figured out how it could be done.

Although Rómulo was optimistic, experience told him that the church would not readily accept the new music. Samuel longed to play his guitar in the church. But he didn't want to play the American-style hymns.

When he was sixteen years old, Samuel made an initial effort to introduce his own style of worship music. He composed several songs, recorded them on cassette and then sent them to Radio Amauta, a Christian radio station that broadcast programming in Quechua. He hoped that one day he would hear his music going out on the airwaves to his Quechua people. But it wasn't meant to be.

He never heard the music, and the tapes were never returned. "I'm sure they probably burned them," he confessed to Rómulo.

Now, with the Messengers of God formally organized, Samuel, Walter, and the others began to build their repertoire of music. With their guitars, *charangos* (a small guitar-like instrument), pan flutes of all sizes, and drums, the group was beginning to develop its own recognizable sound.

One night Walter burst into the practice session and announced, "Hey, we've been invited to perform over in Huanta." The members glowed with excitement. Finally they would have a chance to show off their new music.

At the small Presbyterian church in Huanta, a nearby city, they stood before the congregation playing their beloved music. They hoped the people would be excited to hear the typical Quechua rhythms and melodies played with native instruments—all for the glory of God.

But instead, the congregation sat in a state of shock. Murmurs began to rise out of the gathering. At first they didn't notice, but suddenly someone stood up and threw something at them. Others began to yell, "Music of the devil!" Another shouted, "That's worldly music!" Still others cursed them, "This music is out of the pit of Hell; it's satanic!"

Walter motioned the group to stop playing. Transfixed by the shouting, the musicians didn't know what to do. They had poured their hearts into something radical and different, but it certainly wasn't worldly. The words of the music proved that.

A church elder rushed to the podium. "This music will damage our testimony in the community. We'll be linked with the drunks and unbelievers in a way that will hurt us, not help us," he blared into the microphone.

Walter quickly assessed the situation. This was a turning point for their people and the expression of faith within their culture.

If they could overcome decades of misguided teachings about the role of the Quechua culture in the church, he and the others knew—as Rómulo had often said—that the gospel would more easily find its way into the people's hearts.

Fernando Quicaña, who had accompanied the group, paced back and forth with tears of frustration welling up inside of him. He felt responsible for encouraging these young men to try something new. The congregation's protests grew louder. Some members of the group thought they were going to be lynched. As several men began making their way to the platform, Walter boldly moved to the microphone and pled for a moment of silence.

"Brethren! Brethren, please!" he called out, raising his hands for silence. "Let's not be so quick to judge the music. Remember how the Pharisees in the book of Acts wanted to squelch the apostles? The apostles were trying something radically different from Judaism—Christianity. In the midst of that angry crowd, the Jewish teacher Gamaliel stood up and encouraged the people not to go against God. In the same way, if this style of music is of man, it will soon end. But if this is from God, it will continue no matter how much you oppose it."

The congregation calmed down. Then someone said, "But their music is so worldly."

"It's not worldly," another defended. "Haven't you been listening to their words—they come straight from the Bible." The congregation erupted into another argument.

As the group stood dejectedly on the platform, they knew the concert had ended. Better to let them debate. Quickly they packed their instruments and rushed for the door. As they traveled back to Ayacucho on the bus, they each silently wondered if their music would ever be accepted in the Quechua church.

Samuel later confided to Rómulo, "Our new music brings me much joy. It has given me a new means to worship our Lord."

Rómulo agreed. "We don't want to absorb those words of discouragement from the brothers in Huanta. We know this music has touched something very deep inside of us, and we have to keep going."

Since Rómulo's return to Ayacucho, most of his attention was focused on the translation of the Old Testament. As he worked on the Psalms with Homer Emerson and the other translators, Rómulo realized that these hymns to God could be translated in Quechua in such a way as to be easily set to music. By singing the Psalms, the Quechua people could receive the Scriptures into their hearts whether they could read or not. He worked at putting the Psalms into a meter that could be set to Quechua-style music. Not long after that first performance in Huanta, Rómulo composed a tune for the words from Psalm 23:

Dios Taytalláy, qamllam kanki ñoqallaypa
michiqnillayqa . . .
The Lord is my shepherd, I shall not want. . . .

As Rómulo taught the new song to the Messengers of God, the men quickly joined in. They reflected on the simple words of another shepherd from long ago. Now these shepherds in the Andes lifted their voices to God in praise and adoration. The Lord was the Shepherd of their lives.

A breakthrough finally came for these discouraged young musicians. The Quechua Evangelical Committee held an international music competition. Quechua music groups came from as far away as Ecuador and Bolivia and from all over Peru to compete in it. When the groups held practice sessions before the competition, some members of the Messengers of God went to listen. They were surprised to learn that the musicians had adopted the same style and rhythms they had been working on. When other members of the congregation attended the festival and saw the trend toward Quechua-style worship, they decided to support their own Messengers of God. The festival was a big success. It seemed as though half the city of Ayacucho was caught up in it, and thousands flocked to hear these exciting new indigenous groups. The music festival marked a turning point in the acceptance of Quechua music as a legitimate form of worship in the church.

Soon the Messengers of God received invitations to play throughout the country—weddings, funerals, worship services, all-night prayer meetings. Never before had there been so many opportunities to bring the gospel to the people, many of whom had never heard of the Lord nor had ever set foot inside a church to hear Christian music.

Rómulo set many of his translated Psalms to music and taught them to his friends and the Quechua musicians in churches all over the highland plateau. "Denominations are not the Quechua way," he often reflected. "In fact, these different denominations have done a lot of harm. With all the suffering of our church, one of the ways the Lord is allowing us to renew our sense of community is through our music. The music crosses denominational lines and joins us together."

The Quechua Evangelical Committee (TAWA) embraced the new musical forms and sent groups of musicians with an evangelist into the most remote, hidden corners of Quechua territory. They also sponsored public health programs and provided supplies and assistance to orphanages and to refugees fleeing the terrorism in their mountain communities. In addition they distributed Quechua New Testaments and hymnbooks, and they taught the people how to read through literacy and bilingual education programs. In all these programs they incorporated Quechua culture so that the gospel would freely go forward without the natural barriers that had once denied them a complete understanding of the things of God.

TAWA's pioneering ministry has flourished into a continent-wide outreach encouraging native Christians to embrace the gospel through the perspective of their culture, exploring the applications of music, and teaching the church to care for the humblest member of their social structures.

As music began to play an important role in the Quechua church, Rómulo's concern for theological purity and faithfulness to the gospel prompted him to review all the emerging new music. In all, more than 6,000 new songs were written in the first few years by the proliferating music groups which the Quechua churches now heartily endorsed.

9

Near Miss at Chosica

Arcangel's white pickup sagged with the weight of so many passengers. Rómulo was impatient to get out of Ayacucho and into the lovely mountains that pointed the way toward home. Already they had spent too much of the day preparing. Suddenly he noticed that one of his suitcases was missing. It had the medical supplies he had brought for his people. He searched frantically among the bags and boxes already loaded onto the truck, but it was gone. No one remembered seeing it. First he had lost a bag in Ecuador, then the empty suitcase at the Lima airport, and now this. The gifts he had so carefully picked out and wrapped with pretty bows were evaporating like water into the desert sand.

"Did they take my flowers as well?" Rómulo asked. From Atlanta, Georgia, to Quito, Ecuador, to Peru, and now to Ayacucho, Rómulo had guarded a small bouquet of silk flowers.

"Silk is really great because it looks realistic, and it doesn't wear out," Rómulo had told Arcangel. For months he had been planning just how he would place them at his grandfather's grave as a small symbol of his love. With relief he noted that he still had the bag with the flowers.

As they reached the highway and gathered speed, Rómulo's brother Ruben noted, "Father, we haven't prayed for our trip yet." With all the delays they had finally taken off in such a rush that no one had thought to commend their trip to the Lord's protection. "This is probably why we've had so much trouble getting out of town," Ruben said. "We haven't asked the Lord to be a part of our plans."

Enrique nodded. "Let's pray," he said. "Father in Heaven, You know the importance of this trip to Chakiqpampa. You know the needs of Your people in our home village—how they need Your encouragement and some preaching from Your Word. . . ." As he prayed, the others murmured in agreement. "Also, Lord, You are well aware of the dangers on the road. Encamp your angels around us—"

Suddenly Ruben yelled, "Hey! Who threw that bag off the truck?" His eye had caught a movement in the rear-view mirror. "Stop! We need to go back!"

Enrique was annoyed. "Weren't you praying with us, Ruben?"

"Yes . . . with my eyes open, Father," he replied.

Arcangel brought the truck to a stop and began to back up. One of the men in the back hopped off to collect the bag. No one had seen it fly out except Ruben. Strange. But stranger things had happened in the course of his ministry in Ayacucho, Rómulo thought quietly.

Rómulo's return to Ayacucho in 1978 was full of promise despite the unrest in the air. Although political leaflets and placards appeared everywhere on the streets and angry young men and women shouted slogans at the university campus, Romulo's optimism kept him from expecting anything but good for his people. Each morning, as he had done since his childhood, Rómulo would kneel in his bedroom and begin the day with prayer.

With a computer printout of the Quechua New Testament in

front of him, he prayed, "Thank You, God, for allowing me and my family to return to Ayacucho. Bless the work of our hands and protect us from the Evil One."

Since their move to Ayacucho, Rómulo, Donna, and their son Rumi were living in a guest house on the property of the Wycliffe Bible Translators' Quicapata center. He and Donna began to work with other church leaders to train outreach teams in agriculture, literacy, and basic health maintenance. Donna trained health workers, teaching them how to set up rudimentary clinics in surrounding villages. At the clinics the people had access to medical assistance for a low fee. Here the health workers met the physical as well as the spiritual needs of the people.

Shortly after Rómulo returned to Peru, the Bible society asked him to help on a revision of the first draft of the Old Testament. Impressed with his work on the New Testament, they felt his participation was crucial to completing the entire Bible in the same idiomatic style. A team of translators and language helpers was assembled, led by veteran Bible translator Homer Emerson and Rómulo.

Over the next two years, Rómulo and Donna would often travel down to Lima to meet with the team. Though Rómulo had considered moving to Lima for the sake of the translation work, his heart was among his people in Ayacucho, and he found it difficult to separate himself from them.

Rómulo's arrival in Ayacucho attracted a lot of attention. As he and Donna rode around in their Jeep ministering to the people, many were struck by their compassion. Even the most insignificant shoeshine boy on the street captured Rómulo's attention; no one remembered that once Rómulo had plied the same trade here. No one except Rómulo could have known that a simple gesture of kindness from a stranger would send a shoeshine boy's spirits soaring.

Rómulo's popularity became a matter of concern for followers of the emerging Shining Path revolutionary movement. Cell groups organized by Professor Abimael Guzman had multiplied throughout the mountain communities like a terminal disease. His disciples were biding their time. On May 18, 1980, the Shining Path burst into international prominence when a band of youths burned the ballot boxes and voting lists in Chuschi, a village in the department of Ayacucho. The insurgents, many of them Quechuas, believed that Peru needed to be conquered with a Maoist strategy that would begin in the rural communities and slowly encircle and strangle the cities.

Guzman, however, directed the revolution from a distance. Plagued with skin rashes aggravated by the arid highlands around Ayacucho, Guzman was forced to move to Lima. There he became the most-wanted man in Peru. Over the next twelve years, the Shining Path would cause more than $22 billion in damages to Peru's infrastructure, directly or indirectly cause the deaths of more than 25,000 people, and spread a brand of terrorism that would shake the country to its foundations.

Police launched a massive manhunt that would last for more than a decade. However, Guzman and his cadre of deputies eluded police dragnets, and he took on godlike proportions. The man seemed untouchable.

Guzman's wife, Augusta de la Torre, served as his second in command until 1988 when she dared to challenge him on a question of policy. Soon afterward she died, apparently of suicide. But Shining Path observers suspected that Guzman had persuaded her to kill herself "for the good of the Party."

Though they couldn't find him, security forces in Lima believed he was nearby because this was one of the places where he could get expert medical assistance for his physical ailments. And though he could not spend significant time with his disciples in the highlands, his writings circulated from cell group to cell group, and highly organized networks carried out his commands.

During the organizing period in the 1970s, most Peruvians were unaware of the festering problems in Ayacucho. Twelve years of military rule in Peru had finally ended with a democrat-ically elected president and the prospects of a new era of eco-nomic growth and freedom. Few Peruvian leaders wanted to acknowledge the terrorism developing in Ayacucho, fearing the military would once again take control of the country and impose its strong-arm tactics.

Rómulo's relationship with international organizations brought many threats from Shining Path. His work on the trans-lation of the Old Testament was equally disturbing to them. This was not the message they envisioned for the villages they hoped to conquer with their ideology.

One day Rómulo and Donna left Ayacucho for an overnight trip to a distant village. They often traveled to remote Quechua hamlets to check portions of newly translated scripture with the Quechua villagers. While they were gone, a squad of heavily armed young men moved near the mission compound and pre-pared to attack. On command, they fired their machine guns into the gate with a deafening RATATATAT and forced their way into the compound. They surrounded Rómulo's house and began banging on the door.

"Come out, Rómulo. We know you're in there," the com-mando yelled.

Ruben, left in charge, sprang out of bed in terror. He had to hide before they stormed the house, he thought, and he scram-bled for the attic. The banging continued and shots were fired into the air, but after more than an hour, the commandos finally drifted off into the night.

When Rómulo returned and heard about the incident, he knew in his heart that the city was no longer safe for him or his family. If it were not for his family, he would have chosen to stay with his people. Yet if he were killed, who would push for the completion of the Bible in Ayacucho Quechua? How could his people be truly free if they didn't know God? And how could they know God if they didn't have His words in their language?

There was no other choice than to pack everything and move to Lima where he could live and work in peace.

Zoila and her sister offered to accompany the family on the trip. After several hours of driving the winding roads down the western slope of the Andes, Rómulo stopped the car in a clearing to let everyone stretch their legs. They piled out of the vehicle. And as they did, Zoila suddenly turned and looked back at the car.

"What's that, Rómulo?" she asked as she pointed toward the mirror.

"What do you see, Mother?" Rómulo replied with a puzzled look. He didn't see anything unusual with the car.

"It's so clear to me," she said and proceeded to describe a red hammer and sickle that had appeared in the mirror. No one else in the family had seen the vision. Again Rómulo asked her to describe what she had seen. When she finished, Rómulo was certain that she was describing the hammer and sickle symbolizing the Communist Party.

What are you trying to tell us, Lord? Rómulo prayed in his heart. He didn't want to show his concern, but he felt that the Lord was warning them about something that lay ahead and preparing them. They all returned to the car, and Rómulo eased the Jeep back onto the highway.

Before long, Rómulo slowed down to circle around a sharp curve. As they rounded the curve, suddenly everyone gasped. Ahead the road was blocked by young men and women carrying red flags.

"*Senderistas!*" Rómulo whispered to himself. He was sure Shining Path rebels had set up the roadblock—a tactic becoming increasingly common. If a motorist had the misfortune to be stopped at one, anything could happen. A war tax might be levied, a foreigner or a representative of the government would be shot, a young boy might be forcibly recruited into the rebel forces. The young revolutionaries were totally unpredictable and ruthless. Now Rómulo knew why the Lord had given his mother the vision of the hammer and sickle.

Unless he found a way around the roadblock, Rómulo feared that he would be forced to turn over his wallet—an unwelcome prospect considering their meager income. But what frightened him more was that Donna, a tall statuesque blonde with piercing blue eyes, would draw their attention immediately. How could he explain to them that she had no connections with a foreign government—that she was just as Peruvian in her heart as they were?

In a split-second decision, Rómulo yelled out, "Hold on!" And with a roar of the engine, he geared into four-wheel drive and raced out into the open space around the roadblock. The *Senderistas* scrambled for their weapons and fired warning shots, but Rómulo was determined not to stop. There was too much at stake.

Everyone in the Jeep screamed in fear as they careened down the hillside, narrowly missing trees and boulders. Minutes later at a safe distance, Rómulo steered the vehicle back onto the two-lane highway, and everyone breathed a sigh of relief. Rómulo said nothing. He set his eyes on the road ahead and drove as fast as he could toward Lima.

An hour later, they drove into the village of Castro de Virreyna. Rómulo thought about reporting the roadblock to the police, but he decided against it when he remembered that a *Senderista* strategy was to wear military or police uniforms as a disguise. He had no way of knowing if they had taken over this village. So he reluctantly drove past the police station. As they rounded a corner on the road leading out of town, they came upon a burning lake of gasoline. A heavy truck had been deliberately overturned and set on fire. Acrid smoke and fire filled the air, and out of a cloud of smoke hundreds of people began running down the road toward their car.

"We're trapped," Rómulo shouted. "Those terrorists in the mountains must have had a radio. Help us, Lord!" The others in the car began praying all at once. Rómulo tried to back up, but the car had been blocked off. So once again he jammed the gear into four-wheel drive and veered off the road onto a rocky embankment. With the engine whining, he accelerated and raced the vehicle down the mountainside, around the lake of fire, skillfully maneuvering around bushes and large rocks until he finally reached a safe stretch of highway.

As they drove on, Rómulo prayed silently, *Will we be able to make it, Lord? Please send Your angels to clear a path before us if it is Your will for our lives."*

Just as he finished telegraphing his prayer to God, it happened again. The road ahead was flooded. On one side was the sheer face of the mountain—on the other a steep drop-off.

Rómulo gently slowed the car to a crawl and began to ease through the muddy water. Suddenly a large truck appeared from the opposite direction. Unable to stop, the truck slammed into the Jeep and began pushing it toward the cliff. Rómulo gripped the steering wheel and prayed. Everyone around him was screaming and crying. Like a bulldozer, the truck kept pushing the car closer to the edge. Rómulo's mother began rebuking the truck in a loud voice, commanding it to stop in the name of the Lord Jesus. In a split second the truck came to a dead stop just long enough to allow Rómulo to steer around it safely to the other side.

With a sigh of relief, Rómulo once again praised the Lord for His protection on what was turning out to be the most frightening trip of his life.

The Sauñes finally arrived in Lima and settled into temporary mission housing. Rómulo unpacked his books and resumed working on the Old Testament. Here he could work in safety, but a constant stream of visitors from Ayacucho and other regions affected by terrorism interrupted him.

Word had spread among the Quechua Christians in Lima that Rómulo was now among them. Pastors would ring the doorbell early in the morning or late at night seeking advice and companionship. "Brother Rómulo, how would you advise me to help the widows and orphans in my village?" "Rómulo, I'm straddling a fine line with the military pulling me one way and the Shining Path pulling me the other way. What should I do?"

Now a pastor's pastor, Rómulo turned no one away, but always patiently tried to give the person an answer from God's Word. The discussions were long and tiring. Soon the Saúñes knew they would have to find a larger, more secluded place to live and work.

The family moved into a small apartment in Lima, but night after night the living room floor became the resting place for dozens of Quechua Christians fleeing terrorism. Some mornings Donna and Rómulo would find their small apartment literally filled wall to wall with people who needed a temporary place to stay.

"We've got to get more space," Rómulo said to Donna one day. "I've been praying early in the mornings asking the Lord to give us a place where I can work in peace with the translation team. We can't delay getting the Word of God into the hands of our brethren up in Ayacucho."

"Honey, maybe God will give you the desires of your heart," Donna said. "Perhaps He will provide a center where you can translate the Bible and train others to minister to the Quechua people." So the two began searching.

At times Rómulo had to return to Ayacucho to meet with the church and to take care of family business. It saddened him to learn that shortly after he and Donna had moved off the Wycliffe property, the army had moved in and converted the little oasis into a military encampment. This was only the beginning of the militarizing of Ayacucho, which would plunge the church into a nightmare that would last for many years.

Ruben and Rómulo observed the compound from a distance. Rómulo barely recognized the property. The beautiful rose bushes had been trampled and the tall eucalyptus trees ripped down and cut up for firewood.

"Ruben, what happened to all the bushes and the fruit trees?"

"They were afraid the terrorists would hide behind them, so they chopped them down."

The property was ideally suited for a military stockade. The flower-lined lawns now served as helicopter pads, and the parking lot was filled with transport trucks and other military paraphernalia. An ancient colonial wall ran the length of the hilltop property, but sections of it were being dismantled to set up guard posts.

"Where's my dog?" Rómulo suddenly asked.

"The army cooks butchered him yesterday and fed him to the soldiers," Ruben said with a shake of his head. "I couldn't stop them."

"And what about Turquesa, your dog?" Rómulo pointed to Ruben's beloved silver German shepherd in the front yard.

"Turquesa is really smart so they are training her to search for dynamite," he explained. "So I've lost my dog as well. She's theirs now."

The military was entrenched in what had once been the site of many wonderful moments in Rómulo's life. The war was beginning to take its toll, and it would leave no one untouched.

Through networking among the missionaries in Peru, Rómulo and Donna soon learned about an ideal property in Chosica, about an hour's drive east of Lima. A large house stood on an upper level where Rómulo and the family could live. On the lower level were an office building and a small chapel.

The missionary couple who owned the property was about to retire and wanted to sell before returning to the United States. The Sauñes were definitely interested—though unsure about the location—so they agreed to move into a small guest house while the missionaries made final plans for their move home.

The property was certainly suitable for what the Sauñes had in mind—a ready-made conference center for training, translating, and editing, as well as a haven for their many visitors. So they decided to stay. The looming question was how to find the $20,000 down payment. At this time they lived on less than $500 a month, so to accumulate that large sum seemed impossible.

"We've got a big God," Rómulo reminded Donna as they prayed and began to ask the Lord for guidance. The impossible from the human perspective is always possible from God's perspective. After discussing their financial situation with the missionaries, Rómulo and Donna agreed to take over the property for a monthly payment of $500. But even that seemed impossible to Rómulo.

However, in the weeks that followed, Rómulo and Donna began writing to their friends and supporting churches in the United States. Through them the Lord provided the additional funds needed to make their monthly payments and live as comfortably as before. They never missed a payment, and in a few short years the property was completely paid for.

While Rómulo and Donna set up shop, the stream of refugees from the highlands kept them aware of the intensifying revolutionary struggle. The brethren often arrived penniless and panic-stricken by the horrors they had witnessed. Many of the fields had been mined, making it dangerous to plant crops or attend to those that were ready for harvest.

In Chakiqpampa where Rómulo's grandfather, Justiniano Quicaña, still lived and carried on a powerful Christian witness, the believers often got caught in the cross-fire between terrorists and soldiers. Young revolutionaries would descend on the village and demand the allegiance of the townspeople. Despite what had happened to Teofila, Justiniano felt that, as patriarch and elder statesman of the community, he couldn't allow anyone to destroy the peace. But the situation was rapidly unraveling. The military, in hot pursuit of the rebels, would arrest anyone who appeared to aid the enemy; the rebels would kill anyone who appeared to be aiding the military. What was one to do?

Soon after the rebels burned down the Quicaña home and the church next door, Justiniano rebuilt both bigger and better than before. God even provided better benches and new musical instruments, which Justiniano proudly pointed out to visitors and members alike. His sermons were filled with fire, warning his flock to be wary of Shining Path ideology. To the dismay of the revolutionaries, the young people continued to attend the church in large numbers.

One day a squad of masked rebels or *Senderistas* galloped into Chakiqpampa, reining in their sweat-lathered horses outside the Quicaña home.

"Don't preach to the young people, Justiniano. Or it's your life," they warned.

Justiniano stood in the doorway and lectured them, "I've got to be faithful to my Lord Jesus Christ and His Word."

"Well, you've been warned," the leader said as he turned and galloped away with his deputies. The gauntlet had been thrown down. Everyone knew that Brother Justiniano and the Shining Path were headed for violent confrontation.

Terror ruled the days and nights in the Quechua villages—and people had a sense of foreboding they had never experienced before. At night people would sit around their fires and listen for the muffled steps of approaching terrorists. During the day the presence of the army struck fear into their hearts, for they knew that they would have to answer to the rebels for appearing to support the soldiers who passed through their towns. Everyone in Chakiqpampa knew someone who had been killed or who had disappeared in a military sweep, never to return home again.

Like piercing lights in gathering darkness, Justiniano, now eighty-three, and his wife Teofila, seventy-six, refused to move away and leave their frightened brethren behind. Though their children and grandchildren had long since moved away, they knew they could call on them at any time.

On December 10, 1989, the town was electrified by the news that the *Senderistas* were headed their way. Most of the villagers fled to neighboring towns and communities, but Justiniano thought to himself, *I'm just an old man. What would they want with me?* So he instructed his wife to take refuge with friends, not wanting her to chance the nightmare of another kidnapping.

The next afternoon eight hooded men rode into town and went straight for the Quicaña home. Justiniano eased open the door.

"Come with us," the leader barked pointing his rifle at the elderly man with the flowing white beard.

"I'm old," Justiniano protested. "Leave me alone. I don't need to obey you. I'll do as I want."

"You're the leader of those miserable Christians," the leader shouted in Quechua. "You've turned your friends, the police, and the foreigners, against us. We know how to deal with your kind."

With a nudge from their rifles, the *Senderistas* forced Justiniano to walk down the road. They came to an open area where some two hundred insurgents waited, some mounted on horses.

"So you're a leader, huh?" the commander taunted. "How well do you hear without that little gadget you got from the foreigners?"

"Yeah, that's how you talk with the military—it's really a radio, isn't it?" another terrorist screamed at Justiniano, who remained silent. Then the terrorist reached up and yanked out Justiniano's hearing aid, flinging it to the ground and crushing it with the heel of his boot. Others began beating Justiniano with clubs.

"Stop," Justiniano pleaded. "Can't you see that I'm your brother? We're all Quechuas." The blows only came harder.

Horrified, a number of villagers stood by weeping as they saw their pastor trying to dodge the blows. "Stop it!" someone yelled out. "He's an old man." But the rebels didn't seem to hear.

Bruised and bleeding, Justiniano pled, "Please stop. You're acting like savages who have no pity or no God. You can attack my body, but you can't touch my soul. Never!"

The words only infuriated the terrorists. As Justiniano raised his hand to deflect the blows, a rebel slashed him with a knife. Blood spurted out. Justiniano doubled over and fell to his knees, gripping his wounded hand.

"We'll show you, old man, what we think about your preaching," the commander sneered. He gripped the blade of his knife and reached for Justiniano, grabbing him by his hair and forcing his head back with a snap. Justiniano's mouth hung open. With a swift move, the commander yanked out Justiniano's tongue and slashed it off. He held the tongue high for everyone to see. Justiniano moaned.

Then another terrorist roughly pushed him onto his back. Handful by handful, he plucked out Justiniano's flowing white beard. Loud moans escaped the old man's bleeding mouth. Then with a final stroke of indignity, the terrorist took his blood-drenched knife and scalped off Justiniano's hair.

Pinning the old man to the ground, another rebel reached for his knife, and, like the Inca priests of ancient days, he plunged it savagely into Justiniano's chest. With a broad stroke he ripped open the chest. Shouting wildly, he reached in and tore out Justiniano's still-beating heart. The blood fanned out in a spray of red, shocking the *Senderistas* into silence.

"Oh, my God! Save us!" a man screamed.

The assassin flung the heart onto the ground and screamed at the villagers, "If anyone buries this body, he'll suffer the same fate! Let the sun rot this body for everyone to see."

Then the squad of killers turned and solemnly rode out of town in single file, their rifles slung over their shoulders and their blood-stained knives sheathed at their sides.

Justiniano's wasn't the only death that day. In a violent rampage, the insurgents rode through the surrounding villages and killed forty-five others.

After the rebels had left Chakiqpampa, Teofila hurried back to the village, only to find her husband lying lifeless in a pool of blood. In shock, she collapsed next to him and mourned throughout the night. No one wanted to come near for fear of suffering the same fate. The following morning she shuffled back to the house, but it was burned to the ground. Nothing remained. Even the cows and the horses and the sheep were gone.

When news of the murder reached Ayacucho the next day, Enrique Sauñe, Justiniano's son-in-law, went to Chakiqpampa to arrange for the burial. As they stood around the coffin in the quiet country cemetery, no one from the immediate family wore black, though tradition called for it. "Wear white!" Justiniano had once told his family. "I'm going to Glory! It's a victory celebration, not a defeat!"

In accordance with Peruvian law, the military arrived a week later to verify reports of Justiniano's death. Eight soldiers marched into town and asked to see the widow. Teofila cautiously approached them. Since Justiniano's death, she had maintained a silent vigil underneath a tree, wrapped in a blanket which she had managed to salvage from the rubble of her ruined home.

"We need to see the body to fill out our report," the squad leader said to Teofila.

"Why? He's been dead for a week already. What's the point?" Teofila protested.

"The law is the law, and our papers must be filled in. We can't do it without seeing the body," the soldier insisted. "Come on, take us to the grave site now!"

Teofila began shuffling toward the cemetery. She wondered how they would get the body out of the fresh grave. When they arrived, the answer soon became clear. "Here's a shovel for you," the soldier said handing her a small shovel lying nearby.

"Young man, what am I supposed to do with this shovel?"

"Start digging," he ordered.

Until that moment Teofila had managed to stem the tide of tears. At the thought of digging up the grave of her husband, they began to stream down her face. How much more would she have to suffer in this terrible war she didn't understand?

With each shovelful, Teofila came closer to the coffin. The men chided her and prodded her along, "Can't you work any faster?" No one lifted a hand to help her. She continued to dig. Finally the coffin was clear enough for them to open it and "accurately fill out their paperwork." They uttered no word of thanks to Teofila. Instead the commander demanded a sheep in payment for his work.

"Can't you open your eyes and look around you?" Teofila cried. "The Shining Path destroyed my home. I'm sleeping under a tree. Get out of here! I have nothing left to give you!"

The men left as Teofila sobbed and fell to the ground.

10

To Walk Where Jesus Walked

After stopping to recover the lost bag that had mysteriously flown out of the back of the pickup, Rómulo and his family got on their way again, anxious to reach Chakiqpampa before darkness. They knew better than to try to walk the mountain trails after dark. Ever since terrorism had gripped the countryside, no one dared venture out.

Arcangel happened to look down at his gas gauge. It was empty! He groaned inwardly. In the bustle of getting ready for the trip, he had completely forgotten to fill the tank. He shot a glimpse over at Rómulo, and their eyes met. Another delay! Arcangel pulled into a gas station he always used on his way to Chakiqpampa, but the station was closed. A caretaker called out to him, "There's an open station over by the airport."

Rómulo groaned. The airport was clear across town, nowhere near the direction they were traveling in. "What's going on here?" he blurted out. "Why can't we even get out of town?" The tone of frustration was unusual for him.

Years before, Rómulo had been just as eager to get to another part of the world—Israel. In the course of translating the Old Testament he was sorely aware of his lack of knowledge about the land. Descriptions were important to the Quechuas, and the photographs Homer Emerson showed him just didn't give the detail needed to make the Scriptures come alive. He couldn't have imagined how the Lord would provide a way for him to learn more about the Promised Land.

With the purchase of the property in Chosica, Rómulo and the translation team could devote themselves full time to the work. Although portions of the Old Testament had been translated into Ayacucho Quechua since the 1950s, the literalness of the translations deeply concerned Rómulo and other church leaders. It was finally determined that the Old Testament could not be revised, but a completely new translation was needed.

Old Testament translations often take decades to complete, Rómulo knew. The war was beginning to rage in the mountains of Peru. He didn't have decades; he wanted the complete Bible available to his suffering people as soon as possible. Also Homer Emerson was well beyond retirement age, and his mission was urging him to return to the United States. Homer suffered from a heart condition that limited the number of hours he could work at the translation desk each day. Often the team would have to stop at noon to allow him several hours of rest. Then they would continue working long into the night.

Rómulo attacked the translation work with unprecedented urgency. Hour after hour he pushed the team through chapter after chapter, book after book. From time to time, translated material would be sent to Donna at their home on the upper level. She would take the pages and, together with a young woman named Dorcas Céspedes, would key the new material into the computer. From morning until late in the evening the translators lived in a controlled environment, lost in a sea of Bibles and commentaries—Spanish, English, Hebrew, Greek, Aramaic.

"What kind of mountain is Mount Sinai? What size is it and what altitude?" Rómulo asked at one point. "Is it jagged? Or rounded? Is it a peak? Or is it just a foothill?"

Homer Emerson scratched his head as he looked at the Hebrew text for the book of Exodus. His sixty-plus years had taught him a lot about the Scriptures. Across the table Rómulo Saúñe sat expectantly with the other team members.

"The text doesn't say anything about the altitude or the shape of the mountain, Rómulo," Homer said. "It just says mountain. Does it make a difference in Quechua?"

To the uneducated the Quechua language may have appeared primitive. The lifestyle of the Quechuas was not very sophisticated, but when it came to describing mountains, the Quechuas were way beyond anything in English, Hebrew, or Greek. Those languages had only a few words for describing mountains.

"In Quechua we've got dozens of words for mountain," Rómulo explained. To capture the sense of the text he needed to understand the appearance and the altitude. "These books are great but so inadequate when it comes to telling what we need to know about these mountains."

As the weeks went by, this dilemma and many others requiring descriptive terms became more and more problematic. Pictures, commentaries, historical books were inadequate. No one sitting around that table had been to the Holy Land.

"Oh, to walk the streets of Jerusalem and see it all with my own eyes," Rómulo said with a sigh. He wanted to walk where the great prophets and kings of the Bible had walked. At his early morning prayers, Rómulo began asking the Lord for the resources to travel to Israel. The Saúñes even included the idea in a letter they wrote to their prayer partners in the United States.

Miles away from Peru, in a town near Dallas, Texas, Mary Adams was also spending time in prayer. Shortly after receiving the Saúñes' letter describing the progress of the Old Testament translation, Mrs. Adams became seriously ill. As she lay on her deathbed, the Lord prompted her to write out a check for $2,000 to cover Rómulo's trip to Israel.

When the check arrived, Rómulo's spirits soared. The Lord had once again provided a way to fulfill his innermost desires. He flew off to Israel in the spring of 1984.

"In a few moments we'll be landing in Tel Aviv," the El Al Airlines pilot announced. "Welcome to Israel." The air seemed to tingle with excitement. For many of the passengers this was their first visit to the Holy Land.

One of the passengers quietly put away his Bible and reached for his backpack and hat. Rómulo didn't have lots of luggage for his two-week trip to Israel. Instead he brought an open heart, a pair of sturdy shoes, and his trusty *quena*, the Quechua flute that had traveled the world with him.

Early one morning Rómulo jostled through the crowds in the narrow streets of Old Jerusalem. The tight archways and the bustle of the crowd reminded him of the streets of Cuzco, Peru. Even the bleating of sheep and goats sounded familiar. Rómulo smiled as he watched shepherds poke at their sheep to move them along. *How many times I've redirected a wayward sheep with a poke of my staff,* he thought.

Rómulo studied the sheep for some time and made careful notations in a small notebook. These sheep were different from those at home. Some had floppy ears and others had ears that stood straight up. These distinctions were important because the descriptive words he would use in the Old Testament would be different in Quechua.

As Rómulo moved through the city, he noted the cobblestones in the streets and the stone-work in the houses and walls. His Inca ancestors had built similar structures throughout the Andes. The stones in Jerusalem were cut to size as in Peru, but these seemed more finished and squared. Rómulo made a note of these minute differences.

With care not to violate any cultural taboos, Rómulo walked gingerly into the area of the western Wailing Wall. This was one of the few ancient structures left from the days of King Solomon. "My ancestors would have left the rough round shape to the stones," Rómulo said to himself. "They wouldn't have squared the edges." He estimated the size and weight of the stones and marveled at the effort it must have taken to set them into place. Of course, similar questions came from outsiders when they walked the streets of Cuzco, once the home of The Inca.

As Rómulo observed the Orthodox Jews near the Wailing Wall, he noticed that as they prayed, they wore prayer shawls wrapped around their shoulders and attached black boxes of phylacteries around their foreheads. The laws of Deuteronomy resonated with new life for him. "I've never understood the reason for those laws, and now I can at least visualize those passages."

The language of the Israelis also fascinated Rómulo. Through the years he had learned Spanish, but his English was still quite limited. Most of the time he communicated with sign language, often a frustrating experience. But his outgoing personality provided plenty of opportunities to meet Jew and Arab alike.

One day as he walked around Jerusalem, he wandered into a compound that looked like a hotel. The innkeeper greeted him in Hebrew. Immediately Rómulo began indicating with sign language that he needed a place to stay. When he failed to make himself understood, he switched to Spanish, and much to his surprise the innkeeper responded in kind, though with a thick accent and a limited vocabulary.

"This is a hotel for students," he explained. "But you can stay here if you'd like to."

Rómulo checked into a room, and the students in the hotel took an immediate liking to the South American. In the hotel dining room the innkeeper announced to the student guests, "We've got a visitor from Peru, South America. He's related to the ancient Incas and has come to visit our country. I've asked him to share with us about his life back in Peru and to tell us why he has come to visit us here in Israel."

Everyone watched the raven-haired visitor who smiled animatedly as he was introduced. As he began to speak, Rómulo's charisma drew them in, and they prodded him with questions. The innkeeper was employed to translate.

Rómulo smiled and began telling them about his people and the great love he had for the words of the Bible. He told them about the violence permeating the villages back home and the brutal way in which many of his friends and even family members were murdered by this newly emerging revolutionary group. Tears welled up in his eyes as he told about the suffering of his people. The students nodded gravely. They understood a few things about terrorism as well.

Then Rómulo turned the conversation to spiritual matters and talked about how for years the descendants of his Inca ancestors had lived in bondage. But, he said, God was doing a new work in their hearts through the Bible. He explained how he had translated the Psalms into Quechua in such a way that the people now sang the Psalms, much like the Israelites had in Old Testament days.

Then he began to ply the students with questions of his own. What were they studying? What was life for young men like in Israel? Did they have families?

The conversation went back and forth until finally a student asked, "But, Rómulo, tell us why you're here in Israel now? Why have you come such a long way?"

Rómulo began, "I've been translating the Scriptures for my people. But I've been stymied by many of the descriptions such as the shape and height of mountains. We have many words to describe these things, and I want to be as accurate as possible.

"But I find you all so interesting. You have such a love and devotion to the Scriptures," he continued, speaking to the students of the Torah. "Friends, God loves you and appreciates your devotion to His Word. But there is a Man who fulfilled all the prophecies in the Torah. His name was Jesus Christ. He was born of a virgin in the city of Bethlehem. Your study of the Scriptures would have greater meaning if you would accept Jesus as your Messiah."

Amazingly no one threw Rómulo out of the hotel. Others had tried to come and give them this simple message, but the guests wouldn't hear it. Perhaps it was because no one had approached them with the humility they sensed in Rómulo. The innkeeper turned to Rómulo and said, "If you had been any other outsider, we wouldn't have even talked with you. But you have such a kind way of sharing these things about your Messiah it has meant a lot to us."

Rómulo went back to his room praising the Lord for the opportunity to witness to Jewish people about the Messiah. He stayed at the hotel for several days, and the students took him to see the sights around the city.

Soon Rómulo was on his way again, hopping on buses or walking from one village to another. What a joy it was to walk the roads of such an ancient land. Here the Savior had walked and talked with people with such compassion. And as Rómulo traveled to various historical sites, he took careful notes that would enrich his Old Testament translation work.

For his meals Rómulo would purchase pita bread and cheese in the marketplaces where he would strike up conversations with the shopkeepers in his limited English.

To capture a sense of the ministry of Jesus and life on the road, Rómulo decided to walk out into the Sinai Desert. For several nights he slept under the stars. Until then he hadn't realized how cold the desert was at night. He carefully noted that fact in his notebook.

The land of Israel was full of stark contrasts for Rómulo. In some regions the grass grew rich and green, great citrus groves stretched for miles, and pastures were dotted with large herds of sheep. But other regions were barren and carved with craggy mountains and cliffs.

Rómulo was bursting with new knowledge. He longed to share his experiences with someone who understood Spanish, and he was beginning to feel a bit homesick.

One day as he set out on a hike up Mount Carmel, he stopped for a rest at one of the turnouts in the trail. He was discouraged. Often lost and unable to communicate with those around him, Rómulo felt tired and lonely. When he had tried to order a glass of water at a roadside stand, he had been served goat's milk instead. Wasn't there anyone in Israel who could talk with him?

He kicked a rock with his toe and continued hiking up the mountain. Moments later a man in flowing Arab-style robes overtook him. "*Shalom*," Rómulo called out, glad for a chance to practice the few words of Hebrew he had learned.

"*Shalom*," the man replied with a smile. He was tall and strikingly good looking.

As the two walked together, Rómulo began haltingly to tell him he was from South America. The man instantly switched from English to Spanish, shocking Rómulo with the fluidity of his speech.

"Where did you learn Spanish?" Rómulo asked.

"It's just something I picked up along the way," the man replied.

"But you must have lived somewhere in Latin America to have learned Spanish this well. You speak it perfectly," Rómulo said. "What a blessing you are to me. You're the first fluent Spanish speaker I've met since arriving here in Israel."

"You're too kind," the man said with a wave of his hand. As they continued up the trail, Rómulo began telling him why he was in Israel and asking him questions about the mountain they were climbing.

The man began to point out different features on the mountain in a tone of authority. "Rómulo, this is where Elijah confronted the prophets of Baal," he explained. "Excavators have uncovered the ditches the Israelites filled with water for Elijah's sacrifice to God."

Rómulo pointed to the blooming flowers scattered along the hillsides. "Any idea of the name of those plants?" he asked, a natural question for him since his grandfather had taught him much about identifying useful plants and herbs.

"That's the Rose of Sharon," the man responded. And so the conversation continued until they came to a fork in the trail, and the stranger bade Rómulo good-bye.

"Thank you for walking with me," Rómulo said shaking his hand. "I've enjoyed meeting you so much and learning about your beautiful land. God bless you." They separated, and Rómulo turned back to the trail. Then he looked back for a last glimpse of the man, but he was gone! He scanned the landscape. There was no sight of him.

"Where did he go?" Rómulo wondered. "Why did my heart burn with such joy as we hiked up the trail?"

"Will you look at that!" Rómulo exclaimed to no one in particular. Across the road in a field was a small Arab boy perched on a white donkey that was paired with an oxen. The unlikely pair was hooked to an ancient-looking plow, and a man who looked like the boy's father was driving the plow into the ground to make a furrow for planting.

"We never use two different animals yoked together," he thought to himself. The scene took him back to his childhood when he had watched his grandfather work the rocky soil of the Andes in the same way—but with a pair of mules or a pair of oxen attached to a plow. There were many similarities between life in the mountains and life in the land of Jesus.

One morning Rómulo paused at a kibbutz. In exchange for his lunch, he worked alongside the people who lived there. As they picked the fragrant oranges, Rómulo listened to the work songs that measured their pace and kept them all moving along together. The combination of work and community reminded him of the sense of *ayllu* which his people were struggling to regain. Maybe there were things he could learn about the Jewish concept of community that would be helpful in his ministry back home.

Before long it was time to return to Peru. He had walked throughout most of Israel. He had dipped his feet in the cool waters of the Sea of Galilee. He had climbed the mountains described in the Old Testament. And he finally understood what he needed to know to ensure accuracy and a sense of reality in his translation work.

11

The Unanswered Knock

With the gas tank finally filled the members of the Sauñe-Quicaña clan eagerly set off again down the highway toward home. Rómulo hid the frustration he still felt at the delays that had seemingly kept them driving in circles from one end of Ayacucho to the other.

But then ahead they saw that the traffic had slowed to a crawl. "What's going on?" Arcangel asked impatiently. As the pickup rounded a curve, Arcangel grumbled under his breath, "Just what we need. Another police check."

Police were checking identification papers of all travelers on this stretch of the highway. Arcangel could hardly contain himself. "First someone steals our stuff, then the bag flies out of the back, then we can't find gasoline, and now the police check. Why is all this happening to us? Are we ever going to get out of this town?"

But before long they were through the police checkpoint and speeding down the highway. Everyone was excited. For many riding in the truck the trip to Chakiqpampa was a special treat. With all the tensions of the past few years, visits were limited. It had been three years since Rómulo had visited his childhood home.

But no matter where he lived or where he traveled in the world, a part of him remained where he had been raised to fear God and to love his heritage. How grateful he was that God's Word had reached his people. No longer did they have to live in darkness, in fear of the spirits of the mountains, and in fear of death.

After returning from the stimulating visit to Israel, Rómulo was ready to plunge into the task of translating the Old Testament. Rómulo described to the other members of the team the many parallels between Jewish and Quechua culture. They listened intently as he brought Palestine to life for them.

When they neared completion, Rómulo wanted representatives of as many denominations as possible to do the final checking. This would assure him that the Scriptures would be understood and supported by a wide cross section of the Quechuas of Ayacucho. Roman Catholics, Pentecostals, Presbyterians, Seventh-Day Adventists, and Baptists were all consulted. And everyone anxiously looked forward to the completion of the translation as though it were a personal triumph.

Finally the day arrived when Rómulo joyfully announced to Donna, "We've finished the entire Bible. Praise God! Now it's up to the Bible society to publish it."

Rómulo and Donna were exhausted from the marathon effort. It had been some time since they had visited their friends and relatives in the United States. This seemed an appropriate time to take a break and also to deliver personally the computer disks of the New Testament to the Bible society.

In Miami they walked into the Bible society office and handed over their prized possession with a great sense of satisfaction. Then they drove off to visit friends and churches who had supported them through the years. These people would want to know that the long task had been completed.

Several weeks later, Rómulo called the Bible society to check on their progress. The report was not encouraging, "We've got a problem, Rómulo—we're not set up to read your diskettes yet. Besides, the work here is piling up, and we're overwhelmed. We need to tell you that it will take at least a year before we can typeset this project."

"A year!" Rómulo shouted into the telephone. "My people can't wait another year. Thousands of them are suffering because of the conflict in my country. Many are living in fear for their lives. Isn't there anything you can do to speed up the process?"

"No, unfortunately we can't," the Bible society representative said with regret. "We're so short of help here that we couldn't possibly get to this project for at least a year. That's the best we can do."

Rómulo hung up. "I know they're doing the best they can," he explained to Donna, "but it's so frustrating after all the work we did and after we pushed everyone so hard. The thought of waiting breaks my heart."

As they traveled across the country, Donna and Rómulo decided to stop in Dallas, Texas, where the Wycliffe Bible Translators have their International Linguistics Center. Both had studied at the center years before, and they had friends still living and working there. One of these, Bob Chaney, worked in the Printing Arts Department. Donna mentioned to him the problem that lay heavy on their hearts. "Bob, the Bible society in Miami has such a backlog of work they say they won't get to the Ayacucho Bible until a year from now. Is there any way we could do the typesetting here in Dallas?"

Bob checked his calendar. "We're pretty backed up with New Testaments here, but there is some time available while we wait for a New Testament from Papua New Guinea that's scheduled to arrive any day. How would you feel about getting slotted into their time until their New Testament arrives? We've never done a complete Bible so it will be a first for us."

The time slot allotted to them would require them to work with record-breaking speed. Rómulo was surprised by the steps Wycliffe Bible Translators took to ensure an exhaustive and complete check of the Bible. Every chapter and verse was checked and re-checked. One novelty to Rómulo was a computer program that made sure all the verses in every chapter in every book were present. It took the computer three days to thoroughly process the Ayacucho Quechua Bible. The delay was compounded by the Quechuas' rich language. There are hundreds of word combination possibilities for every word. The word to love, *kukay,* has over 360 combinations and differing suffixes. The computer printed out a complete word list of the entire Bible which Rómulo had to check.

As they worked through the computer printouts, Donna and Rómulo often discovered that entire verses had been inadvertently left out. These would have to be re-entered. Sometimes a footnote or chapter title was discovered missing. The work stretched into months.

Finally three months later, the work was done. The entire Bible had been typeset and was ready to be printed. They packed their bags and headed back to Ayacucho.

While Rómulo was pushing the limits of endurance in getting the Bible completed, a very different testing of the limits was occurring in distant Ayacucho. The Shining Path, a name taken from Mao Zedong's description of a shining path toward a socialist utopia, was becoming part of every Peruvian's vocabulary. Professor Abimael Guzman proclaimed in his prolific writings that Stalin's purges and Mao's Cultural Revolution had failed to go far enough—even though millions were slaughtered in the attempts to usher in the perfect Communist society.

When China's Deng Xiaoping flung open the doors to capitalism in late 1980, the citizens of Lima were the first to experience the indignation of the Shining Path. The day after Christmas, shocked Limeños saw a gruesome sight. Hanging from the lampposts throughout the city were the corpses of dogs bearing placards that declared: "Deng Xiaoping, son of a bitch." The scene gave many their first taste of the extremes to which the Shining Path would go to make its point.

The Maoists exploited the weaknesses of the Peruvian military, which was woefully under-equipped to battle the insurgency. The army had difficulty living down the fact that in time of war, up to 40 percent could be expected to desert.

In 1984 the Peruvian government discovered how the Shining Path was financing its revolution. During an anti-drug operation, the military uncovered evidence directly linking the Shining Path with the Colombian drug cartels. At the time, Peru was well on its way to becoming the world's largest producer of coca leaf, the raw material manufactured into cocaine. The Shining Path also imposed "war taxes" on business, which they preferred to call "contributions."

During the 1980s, the Shining Path moved from ideological rhetoric to armed rebellion against the state. Abimael Guzman demanded rigorous allegiance from his foot soldiers. No one dared cross an order that came from Chairman Gonzalo, as he came to be known.

As the armed struggle became national, revolutionaries fanned out through the highlands of Ayacucho and surrounding departments proclaiming the doctrines of Chairman Gonzalo. But the doctrines were lost on the peasant farmers, who never truly took them to heart, much to the frustration of the cadres.

Instead peasants began to flee from the mountains to the large metropolitan centers where they felt protected. Most communities were simply abandoned by the state and left to fend for themselves. In these communities the authority figures were the teachers, the priests, or the evangelical pastors. More often than not, the leader of a village was a pastor or Protestant layworker. From the early days of the Shining Path, the church was never a direct target. But a Christian witness could easily provoke a rebel or a soldier into a rage. Even a plate of food given to the wrong side could bring quick retaliation from the other. There did not seem to be a way to stand one's ground without suffering serious consequences.

Shining Path soon learned that if they were to win over a village or a community, they would have to convince the town leader of their cause. This proved the undoing of pastors who, under threat of death, either gave in or fled. Either way the village was coerced to embrace the foreign ideology.

In the midst of these troubles the Old Testament was finally completed and presented to the Quechua people. On September 3, 1987, Quechua believers streamed down from the mountains by the thousands to attend the joyous celebration. For the first time they held in their hands the entire Word of God in their own language.

Ayacucho was a flurry of activity. Christians paraded through the streets; musicians held outdoor concerts. At city hall the mayor, the bishop of the Roman Catholic church, and representatives of the Peruvian Bible Society took their places at the dedication ceremony, each expressing gratitude for the effort that went into the project.

Rómulo Sauñe, the glue that had kept the translators together, made his way to the podium and stood before the assembly with tears glistening in his eyes. "Brothers and sisters," he began with a slight catch in his voice, "this is a landmark day in our lives. We and other Quechua brethren have suffered much for the gospel of Jesus Christ. But our hope is in the Lord and in the promises He has given us in His Word." He held up one of the new copies of the Ayacucho Quechua Bible. "Now we have the complete Word of God—from Genesis to Revelation—in our own language. Nothing can separate us from His love and His precious words for each one of us. May God bless you as you read His Word and hide it in your hearts."

At the end of the ceremony, Christians crowded around the Bible society booth to purchase Bibles. As they pressed forward, Rómulo realized with consternation that their supplies would soon be depleted.

"How can we get these Bibles out to the people if they can't get a copy today?" he wondered. He knew that many of the brethren had walked great distances from remote communities. As he stood by watching the stacks of Bibles disappear as though into thin air, he suddenly had an idea.

The next week Rómulo went to visit his good friend Al Shannon. As they sat in his Lima office, Rómulo laid out his concern. "Al, the Bible is too expensive for my people. Even at three dollars, it's still too much. What can we do?"

"Look, Rómulo, for every Bible you sell for one dollar, I'll match it with two dollars." Al was convinced that even at the subsidized price, Rómulo would probably sell only a few hundred Bibles. Al could easily cover that many sales with his personal savings.

"That's fantastic, Al!"

When they heard of the plan, the Peruvian Bible Society directors agreed to advance as many copies as Rómulo could sell during the special offer. News of the two-day sale was announced on Quechua radio with plenty of advance notice.

One evening Al told his wife Barbara, "I admire Rómulo's faith. But the country is in shambles. Most of the people don't even have one dollar to spare for food, much less for a Bible."

Several days before the sale, Rómulo and his colleagues, Fernando Quicaña and Walter Parado, loaded up a vehicle with some 5,000 Bibles they were sure would sell out. But on the day before the official sale, Al received an anxious telephone call from Rómulo. "Al, we need your help!"

Al's first thought was that the terrorists had stolen the Bibles. "What's the matter? What's wrong?"

Rómulo laughed. "Nothing's wrong, Al; we've just sold out all the Bibles we brought with us. We don't have any to sell at the sale. Could you send up another 5,000 by tomorrow?"

Relieved, Al replied, "No problem. I'll get those up to you by air first thing in the morning." He called the Bible society and made the arrangements. But then it suddenly struck him, "Wait a minute! I don't have that kind of money! That's going to cost me a fortune. What have I gotten myself into? Help, God."

The next week Rómulo and Fernando came back to Al's office to brief him on the miracle they had just witnessed in Ayacucho. With tears streaming down his face, Fernando said, "Al, the people would do anything to get their very own Bible. They even . . ." and he choked back the tears, "took the clothes off their backs and sold them in the streets to get the money." In one week they had sold an unprecedented 11,000 Bibles, a new record for the Peruvian Bible Society!

And though the sale was officially over, in the coming weeks the people continued trickling into Ayacucho in search of more Bibles. Soon the entire first run of 20,000 were sold out. The Bible society immediately ordered another 20,000 copies. When they arrived, the Quechua church leadership held another sale, and all 20,000 were sold. The Bible society officials shook their heads in disbelief.

But Rómulo knew that the people were ready for God's Word. For more than ten years Wycliffe Bible Translators had organized bilingual education and literacy campaigns, and fostered church growth, preparing the Quechua Christians for such a day. Now they could follow along when their pastors read the Scriptures. Now they were no longer dependent on interpreters to tell them what the Spanish Bible said.

The indigenous Quechua mission TAWA now placed Bible distribution at the top of its ministry priorities. Soon teams of missionaries and itinerant evangelists went out into the Quechua communities to sell Bibles to those unable to come in to the sales. But the missionary journeys were arduous and full of danger. Still the young men were confident that God would bless their efforts and keep them safe.

One of these evangelists, Julian Parejas, was returning to Ayacucho one day from a remote hamlet on an inter-city bus with a bag full of cash from the sale of Bibles. Suddenly everyone in the bus grew quiet. The driver was slowing down. Julian looked out the window, and just ahead he saw a roadblock manned by a squad of masked rebels. His heart sank. Within seconds they came to a complete stop. Everyone was ordered out.

"Women and children, move out of the way," one of the commandos barked.

The rebels lined the men up in front of the bus. "Papers!" the command rang out. Everyone reached for identification documents. "Empty your pockets!" Julian reached for his wallet. He hoped they wouldn't search his bags. But the thought of it filled him with terror. How would he explain the loss of the Bible money?

Suddenly there was a struggle between the bus driver and one of the commandos. Shots rang out. The driver buckled over and fell to the ground. "Get your money out," the commando screamed. The panic-stricken passengers held out their cash. Julian noticed the driver's assistant struggling to pull out a wad of bills stuck in his pocket. The commando couldn't wait. Raising his pistol, he fired at the young man. Bang! A small circle of blood formed on his forehead, and his lifeless body fell to the ground.

The man next to Julian tried to stifle a scream, and the commando casually raised his submachine gun and sprayed him with bullets. Julian was spattered with blood. *Oh, God, I'm next!* he thought. The commando moved toward Julian and raised his gun. Click! He was out of bullets. In a split second the other passengers realized what had happened. With loud whoops and yells, they descended on the commando and pinned him to the ground. Confused, the other two commandos raced off into the bush. Julian stood by the highway trembling with fear. "Oh, Lord," he breathed with relief, "thank You for protecting me."

Though many of the TAWA evangelists had similar deliverances, few could match the experiences of Enrique Saune. Week after week he searched out pockets of abandoned believers in the most isolated communities. Once as he made his way through a high mountain pass, he ran into a group of guerrillas resting by an icy stream. He thought about hiding behind a bush, but it was too late. He had already been seen. As he tentatively approached the fighters, he called out, "Good morning, young people. Are you guerrillas?"

"Yes, sir," someone answered. "We are guerrillas."

Enrique stopped to catch his breath. Then he reached into his bag and pulled out some gospel tracts. "I'm a missionary," he said, and he held up the tracts.

"Who is your boss?" the leader asked with a smirk.

Enrique put his bag down and took out his Bible. Holding it up he said, "My boss is Jesus Christ. I'm fulfilling His commands just as the apostles did."

One of the guerrillas sidled up to him. "I was once a believer. Could I have some of those tracts?"

Enrique smiled and held out a handful of tracts.

"Young people, please behave yourselves," he instructed the guerrillas. "You have a responsibility to be an example for other young people. You may not understand this, but there is a Creator, and there is a Lord of the Universe. One day you will have to answer to Him for your actions."

The guerrillas remained silent. Enrique decided to move on. But before he had gone very far, one of the guerrillas called out, "Are you going to turn us in?"

Enrique paused for a moment. "Gentlemen, I'm just a man like you. I can't turn anyone in. But there is a Lord who one day will judge every man. At this moment He is watching over us and taking notes on everything we are saying here. You must answer to Him."

The house was full of the stillness of the night. Rómulo and Donna were tired. Their Chosica home always seemed like the crossroads of the Quechua community. Though they were glad to make themselves available to the needs and concerns of their brethren, it was good to finally close the door and relax alone. As they prepared to go to bed for the night, Rómulo heard a rap at the door. He hesitated for a moment. Then he called out, "Who is it?"

"Is the pastor there?" a voice asked.

Since the pastor of the Chosica church had long since left, Rómulo replied, "He's not here." Then he heard footsteps walking away. He didn't recognize the voice so he thought nothing more about it.

Early the next morning as Rómulo was finishing his morning prayers, he heard a knock at the door. He opened it, and there stood a young man with a gunny sack over his shoulder.

"Good morning," Rómulo ventured.

"Is the pastor here?" It was the same voice he had heard the night before.

"No," Rómulo replied. "The pastor doesn't live here. Why do you ask?"

"Are you Rómulo Saúñe?"

Rómulo nodded.

"Why didn't you open your door last night? If you had, things would have been quite different. I came by with two of my comrades. We were going to kill you."

Rómulo stared at him wide-eyed. Then with measured words he said, "You're not fighting against me. You're fighting against the God of the universe. That God didn't allow me to open the door."

"But, Rómulo, you know how well we prepare for these assignments. I've worked hard in recent months spying on your church. I even memorized Bible verses so you would think I was part of the congregation. I visited other churches and learned about your methods of worship in order to understand the evangelical mind. I've even taught other comrades how to set dynamite and destroy churches."

Rómulo had never set eyes on the young man before, but he believed him. "Why are you telling me this?"

The insurgent breathed a heavy sigh. "Last night I was tortured by those Bible verses I had learned. They were like a hammer pounding inside my head. Finally I couldn't stand it anymore. So this morning I decided to come and talk to you about your faith, about your God. I don't want to kill you anymore."

Rómulo waved the man into the house. Then he reached for his Bible and sat down next to him. "God is working in your life. You need to repent of your sins. You need to stop wasting your life with the insurgency. It's the only way to stop this torture in your heart."

The young man began to sob. He couldn't speak. But Rómulo gently began to lead him in a prayer. After they had prayed together, Rómulo smiled compassionately, "God's Word says that the angels rejoice when someone enters the Kingdom of God."

The young man reached for his gunny sack. "As an act of celebration, I'd like to give you something." He opened the bag and pulled out a small gun and a handful of ammunition. Then Rómulo understood just how much danger he had been in. But God had protected him and once again spared his family from the Shining Path.

Later that day the converted insurgent stopped by once again at the Sauñe home. "To show you that my repentance is genuine, I'm going to give you a list of places, you know—churches, Bible institutes, and seminaries—that my comrades are going to destroy soon. When we started our armed struggle, we hadn't planned to destroy churches and kill missionaries. But we've changed our strategy. And I'm not in agreement with it."

Then taking a paper and pencil, he began to write down names and addresses. Rómulo was amazed at the depth of preparation the man had received from the Shining Path.

"I'm the director of my section. I was to lead this attack next week. Now I want you to take this list to the authorities so they can save these institutions. I can't do it because I'm afraid the police will arrest me. And when I don't return to my cell group, I'll be accused of being a traitor. Will you help me escape?" he pleaded.

Rómulo nodded. "I'll give you a ride to the next town. Then you can get a head start to safety."

As Rómulo drove back several hours later, he thought, *I've got to protect my family. I'm still on that hit list.* So he decided to move them all to the Wycliffe guest house in Lima, an hour's drive away.

The next day Rómulo met with the leadership of the Evangelical Council of Peru (CONEP). They immediately called state security officers. Soon to his dismay Rómulo was questioned by an agent as though he were an accomplice to the plot.

"You're lying about where this list came from," the agent said with a snarl. "You're from Ayacucho; you're probably part of this conspiracy. We're going to hold you in jail for a few hours while we investigate your story."

Earlier, state security officials had arrested a terrorist who had pretended to be a member of an evangelical church in Lima. When he was searched, they found the same kind of detailed plans as those Rómulo was presenting.

Rómulo's story seemed to check out, so they released him. Two weeks later, he happened to pick up a city newspaper, and there on the front page was a photograph of the young man who had been assigned to kill him. The article stated that police had arrested him on suspicion of being a member of the Shining Path. Several months later, some three hundred inmates believed linked to the Shining Path died in a prison uprising. Rómulo was sure that the young man was among those killed in the shootout.

Some time later Rómulo and Arcangel were visiting Wycliffe missionary Al Shannon. The talk turned to the terrorism spreading in Ayacucho and throughout the remote Quechua communities.

"Al, it's amazing how many have died for the sake of our Lord," Rómulo reflected. "Still we've learned that sometimes God reaches out and protects His people in ways that I just don't understand. Have you heard about what happened to Pastor Jorge?"

Al shook his head. "What about Pastor Jorge?"

"You know that his village is quite a distance from Ayacucho," Rómulo began. "Well, Jorge was the leader of his community. And you know how the Shining Path feels about the leaders of villages—they always try to win them over. One day the Shining Path swept into the village and rounded up the people at gunpoint. They began to lecture. 'Religion is the opiate of the people. You'll remain in your backward ways as long as you hold on to these ancient beliefs. But the words of Chairman Gonzalo will liberate you. You won't be hungry anymore. We won't abandon you like the government has. Everyone will have the right to an education. We'll all live in peace when the revolution triumphs!'"

Then the commander asked, "Who is the leader of this village? Step forward."

Pastor Jorge reluctantly stepped out of the crowd. "Are you willing to accept the authority of the Shining Path in this village?"

The trembling pastor held his head up high and said, "The Lord is my authority. There is no one else."

Turning toward the villagers, the commander yelled out, "This man isn't fit to be your leader. You must only follow the Shining Path. Just so you don't forget, we're going to teach you all a lesson."

He nodded to his deputies. One of them ran off to a nearby house and came out with a straight-backed chair. They pushed Jorge roughly down on it, and the deputies tied him to it.

Some of the villagers tried to escape, but they were surrounded. They hung together, not wanting to witness the horror they knew was coming.

A rebel then began attaching sticks of dynamite to the legs of the chair. "Now everyone must watch to see what happens to those who refuse to submit to the Shining Path." He struck a match, held it for a second like a torch, and then touched the dynamite fuse. The rebels ran for cover.

Suddenly there was a mighty explosion. A cloud of smoke enveloped the scene. The men groaned, and the women began to weep. But then a strong breeze blew the smoke away. There at the epicenter of the explosion sat Pastor Jorge. Alive! The ropes had disintegrated, but he looked as though he were sitting in his own living room. The terrorists slowly lowered their guns. The villagers shouted in relief. Then the commandos turned and fled from the village.

"The rebels have stayed away from that village ever since," Rómulo said.

"That's an incredible story, Rómulo."

"Yes, but that's just one of many amazing interventions by the Lord," Arcangel told Al. "You know, sometimes our people have been called on to make some very difficult choices. Like the time when a congregation of believers was worshiping in a Sunday service and a squad of armed rebels came rushing in.

"'This meeting is over,' a rebel announced. 'No one is going anywhere unless we say so.' He shot a few rounds of ammunition into the air. The pastor stood immobile. The believers cowered in fear. All knew their lives were at risk.

"'We've heard that this group is committed to God,' the rebel continued. 'I want to know who the true believers are. How many here are true believers? How many of you are willing to die for your faith? Raise your hands,' he commanded.

"Fearing they would be slaughtered, most of the congregation remained still. But a small number of believers tentatively raised their hands.

"'Is that all,' the rebel scoffed. 'No one else is a believer in this Jesus?' A few more raised their hands.

"'Well, everyone who didn't raise his hand can leave. The rest of you stay here.' As the people filed out the door, they sighed in relief. They would live.

"Then the guerrillas slammed the door shut and took up their positions behind the commander.

"'Those of you who raised your hands, stop worrying. We're not going to kill you. We just wanted to see who in the congregation believed enough in their faith that they were willing to die for it. That's the kind of commitment we're looking for in the Shining Path. We may not have won you over to our cause today, but we believe you have the commitment it takes to be one of us.'

"Just then they heard a burst of machine gun fire outside the wood frame church. The believers looked at the commander with consternation.

"'Oh, that,' he said casually. 'Those are the people who didn't raise their hands and thought they were getting away. They don't have what it takes to be a part of us. They don't deserve to live.'"

Rómulo and Al stared at Arcangel. They had heard many stories, but not that one. More than five hundred pastors and layleaders had sacrificed their lives in the conflict. Scores of Christians had disappeared, never to be heard from again. No one was left unscathed. The villages were full of widows, orphans, and the aged.

"Do you remember the story Julian Parejas told us about the congregation that was attacked while they were holding a prayer vigil?" Rómulo asked.

Both Al and Arcangel shook their heads.

"It happened in a village at some distance from Ayacucho, near the edge of the jungle. Julian said that about fifty church members were gathered for a prayer meeting. The village had often come under siege, but thus far no one had been killed. That evening, as the believers prayed and worshiped together in their small church, shots rang out, and a voice yelled, 'We've surrounded the church! Come out.'

"The pastor held his hands up for silence as the believers began to panic. 'Wait! Let's pray! God will protect us,' he encouraged his small flock.

"The people fell to their knees crying out to God for His protection. 'Lord, have mercy on us.'

"Again the voice shouted from the distance, 'You're surrounded. Come out or we'll shoot.'

"More shots rang out. The believers huddled together in terror, pleading for deliverance.

"Suddenly a tall, fair-haired man in full-dress uniform got up from one of the chairs and began making his way to the door. The believers stopped praying in midsentence and stared after him. No one had noticed him in the meeting. No one knew him. And he was certainly not one of them. He was a military officer, and he seemed to know what to do.

"As he approached the door, he reached for his sidearm, pulled it out, and held it up for all to see. Then he opened the door and stood in the doorway with his gun at the ready. After a moment of complete silence, the night air filled with screams of terror as the rebels fled into the darkness. When they were gone, the officer returned his gun to its holster and calmly walked away. No one ever saw him again," Arcangel said. "He just disappeared. You see, Al, that's how the Lord is watching over His people."

"Surely that was the presence of the Lord," Rómulo marveled. How would he ever begin to understand all the wonderful things God was doing for His beloved Quechua people?

12

The Rise of the Shining Path

It would take the travelers to Chakiqpampa two hours to reach Paccha, the end of the road. From here they would hike along ancient trails to a highland plateau deep in the mountains.

As they pulled into Paccha, Arcangel suggested, "Let's stop by the local authorities. Maybe they will be willing to watch the vehicle for a few days."

After a few formalities and a bit of negotiating, the pickup was safely stored in back of someone's house. The bags of food, candy for the children, small gifts, and clothing were divided up and loaded on their backs.

Centuries ago the Incas had laid out many of the trails as interconnecting networks of roads leading from the outlying edges of the empire to Cuzco, the home of The Inca, ruler over the vast Tawantinsuyu. Some trails featured small drawbridges over deep canyons, which in times of war could be drawn up. Rómulo wished that kind of protection could keep them safe from terrorism. It wasn't that easy anymore.

When Rómulo and Donna Sauñe returned to Peru in late 1986 after finishing the typesetting of the Quechua Bible, the ruthlessness and boldness of the Shining Path had reached new levels. The cadres simply wiped out anyone or anything that prevented them from achieving their goals. Terror kept people silent. Those who dared to bring charges against the aggressors often disappeared in the night. During 1989, an election year in Peru, more than 120 mayors and other local officials were killed. The Shining Path called for a three-day armed strike. More than a million people fearfully obeyed. The results paralyzed Lima.

On February 14, 1992, Maria Elena Moyano, the deputy mayor of the Lima suburb of Villa El Salvador organized a peace march protesting the brutality of the revolutionary movement. She had been speaking out publicly against the Shining Path. A few hundred people joined in the march, bravely demonstrating against the evil tearing their country apart.

The next day members of the Shining Path tracked down Maria Elena to a backyard barbecue. As her ten-year-old son Gustavo watched helplessly, guerrillas shot her in the face. Then they attached a five-pound pack of dynamite to her body and set it off.

Maria Elena became a national symbol of public resistance to the Shining Path, and Lima's most influential news weekly began calling her "Mother Courage." Two days after her death residents of Villa El Salvador joined in the funeral march chanting, "Shining Path, cowards and assassins, the people will repudiate you!"

Guerrilla supporters shouted back as the mourners marched by, "Shut up or you are next!" The demonstration marked the first time that Lima shantytown dwellers had publicly opposed the Shining Path. It would not go unnoticed.

In June 1990 the Shining Path launched a new wave of terror. One month later Alberto K. Fujimori became President. He vowed to continue fighting against the Shining Path, but in a conciliatory gesture he also offered to negotiate. Nevertheless the violence continued to mount, and the personality cult-building around Shining Path leader, Abimael Guzman, intensified. Some experts suspected that between 5,000 and 10,000 armed rebels formed the nucleus of the rebellion.

The rebels were well paid for their efforts. In comparison to school teachers, who earned about $40 a month, Shining Path foot soldiers received as much as $500, primarily from earnings from "taxes" they levied on drug traffickers.

New recruits would often have to prove themselves loyal to the Shining Path. On one occasion, a squad of *Senderistas* stopped a bus with two French tourists on board. As part of his initiation rite, a fourteen-year-old boy was ordered to shoot them in the head at point blank range. The rebels believed that once a child would kill for them, he would be a member of their cause for life.

Contrary to what the Shining Path cadres believed, many Andean villages repudiated the strong-arm tactics of the revolutionaries and begged the government to give them weapons for their own defense. Isolated Andean communities were rarely protected by the military. The Shining Path's machine guns easily overcame their knives and crudely made spears.

In 1991 President Fujimori instituted a plan for civil defense in the most conflict-ridden regions of the Andes. Through arming civilians, Fujimori hoped to present more resistance to the violence. The ambitious plan placed evangelical Protestants in the middle of an anguishing dilemma—should they take up weapons even as they strived to be agents of love and peace in their communities?

Civil patrols were created. Believers, struggling with the ethics of participation in these patrols, argued for the need for self-defense. Others contended that they must present an unblemished gospel witness. But participation in the patrols was not optional. Whoever refused was branded a traitor or part of the subversion. On the other hand, to join the civil patrol meant to

place one's life at risk. The Shining Path dealt harshly with anyone perceived to be part of the civil defense.

In July 1991 Hilario Mendoza, a Pentecostal pastor from the
Chakiqpampa area, was brutally murdered by the Shining Path.
During a sweep through Chakiqpampa, a band of rebels discovered a small cache of weapons and accused him of organizing the
local civil patrol.

Church leaders in Ayacucho argued that participating in the
civil patrol caused a serious deterioration in the character of local
believers. One leader lamented, "Christians are beginning to
have more faith in their weapons than in God."

Likewise, Christians who took part in social outreach efforts
were common targets of the Shining Path. By meeting the needs
of the poor, aid workers delayed the revolution. The terrorists
forced AMEN (Evangelical Missionary Association to the World)
to close five feeding centers that sustained some 2,700 people in
the most devastated shantytowns ringing Lima. Deputy director
Luis Villar said he believed he would have been killed if he had
disregarded the order.

Nevertheless, a young AMEN missionary named Telmo chose
to live in the squalor of one of the most beleaguered communities. Canto Grande was one big refugee camp. Thousands of
peasants fleeing the violence in the mountains had flooded the
countryside around Lima, forming vast "young towns" that
offered little in the way of services. Even so, many said they felt
safer living nearer the capital.

But the desert climate around Lima is stark and unforgiving.
Makeshift shacks stretched as far as the eye could see. Most people lived without running water, medical care, or electricity.
Squatters or refugees were bewildered by the daunting prospects
of seeking work in the big city. Employers exploited them. In
1991 more than 80 percent of Peru's work force was underem-
ployed. Christian ministries and churches in the capital were

overwhelmed when it came to meeting even the most basic physical and spiritual needs of these people.

Telmo faced constant pressure and threats from the Shining Path for the simplest of tasks he performed, such as building a latrine. When he took in a starving family, Shining Path warned him it was the "wrong move." Nevertheless, Telmo remained in the shantytown determined to be a "Good Samaritan" even if it meant his death.

In October 1991 World Vision terminated its outreach programs in Peru, particularly child sponsorship. Leaders felt they could no longer ensure the safety of their staff members. Nearly 25,000 children had depended on their feeding programs.

While the Peruvian military battled the forces of the Shining Path, believers in the remote Andean hamlets continued trying to sort out how to live for Christ in the conflict. Indigenous organizations like TAWA alone reached out to the Quechua world, as Spanish and foreign missions were virtually banned from the conflict areas.

As some of the Christians learned, the Shining Path knew the church almost as well as it knew itself. Ramon, a nineteen-year-old believer, recalled an incident when he was on his way with an evangelistic team to visit churches in mountain communities. When the team stopped for a rest, one of the team members said, "If we continue on to minister to these pastors and churches, we'll all be killed."

That night several team members wondered where their colleague had obtained this information. The following morning he was gone. Later they learned he was a Shining Path infiltrator. And when they began visiting the villages, they found that some twenty-five churches they had planned to visit had been closed, the pastors either killed or forced out of their communities.

As Ramon traveled around the countryside visiting churches, he was often stopped and interrogated by Shining Path guerrillas. At one point Ramon said he asked one of the rebels, "Why have you killed so many innocent people?"

"What do you mean? We've only killed those who committed immoral and unjustifiable sins against the people—liars, thieves, and adulterers. And we never kill without first issuing a warning. If no change is reported, then the order for elimination is carried out," a guerrilla explained.

As the Shining Path continued to strike out with violence, President Alberto Fujimori's patience was being sorely tested. "What could be done to short-circuit this terrorist group?" he often asked his advisers. The answer finally came April 5, 1992. Fujimori took control of the judiciary and dissolved the Congress. By suspending the Constitution, he seized power and moved aside those he believed obstructed his plans. Several polls were taken to judge the people's reactions. A surprising 75 percent supported Fujimori.

Peruvians felt that their twelve years of democracy had given them only corruption, ineptness, chaos, poverty, disorder, hunger, and malnutrition. So they were ready to try a government willing to use a strong hand.

But the people's hope soon withered. Shortly after Fujimori's dramatic moves, a bus laden with explosives rolled into a police station near Lima, killing a police officer and wounding several bystanders. It also knocked out a local radio station, severely damaged city hall, a library, a school, and a bank. People now realized that the situation could not be quickly changed and that it might get worse.

At TAWA headquarters in Chosica, caring for fleeing Quechuas, providing aid to the displaced, and training leaders to take over responsibilities within the mission was a full-time job. The mission had grown, and with that growth had come added responsibilities. Now president, Rómulo Sauñe used his international influence to draw attention to his people's plight. Despite the uncertain times, the Sa*ñe* home was an oasis of tranquility for Rómulo, Donna, and their three children. But Rómulo felt the Lord wanted them to have another son. However, with Rómulo's busy travel schedule it seemed their plans would have to be put on hold. Rómulo planned to attend a seminar at the Haggai Institute in Singapore. Before he left, Rómulo said to Donna, "We'll have that little boy when I get back."

Two weeks after Rómulo left, Donna realized she was already pregnant. When Rómulo called home to check on the family, Donna told him, "You've missed your chance at a boy. We'll probably have another girl."

After two sonograms, the doctor confirmed that the Sauñes would be having another girl. But Rómulo's mother Zoila scoffed, "Who's the doctor? He's not God. God told me it's going to be a boy." And no one dared argue with her.

Sometime later as Donna delivered her baby in the hospital, the doctor cried out, "Here comes a kusi" (referring to one of their daughters). Then after a pause, he hollered, "It's a boy!"

Rómulo could hardly contain his joy. The couple named their fourth child and second son after the organization dear to their hearts—Tawa.

13

Beyond the
Borders of Peru

As the family began the two-hour trek to Chakiqpampa on foot, Arcangel called out, "I'm going to take the shortcut with Miguel!" And with a final wave the father and son headed off on the more rugged but shorter of the two trails.

The others preferred the easier, more scenic route. Ruben, a filmmaker, wanted to videotape the journey home with all the familiar sites they remembered so well from their childhood. Rómulo pointed out a flock of sheep tended by a young boy on a far off hillside. "Film that, Ruben!" The scene reminded him of the many long hours he had spent roaming the highland meadows with his own flock.

Rómulo reveled in the rugged mountains lining their way. Hours later as the group neared Chakiqpampa, Rómulo could hardly contain his joy. "Mother, this is the place where I imagined the ancient Inca coming to life. I was so scared that I didn't come this way for days. Remember?"

Zoila smiled. She was so happy for her son. He had talked about coming home for so long that now she could hardly believe it was really happening.

People in the outlying houses came out to welcome the Sauñes and the Quicañas back home. Children hopped and skipped alongside, shouting gleefully when Rómulo handed them candy.

Ruben videotaped their arrival. Rómulo had asked him to record their homecoming, as well as signs of the suffering of the believers. The isolated community had so often been the target of the rebels that the villagers no longer slept in their modest homes. The surrounding caves had become their protection in the night. The world needed to know this so they wouldn't forget to pray for them, Rómulo thought.

Then with a turn in the trail and a brisk walk across the meadow, they were home! Rómulo stormed the entrance of his grandmother's house and gave the diminutive Teofila a big hug. Everyone was talking at once. "How are you, Rómulo? Are you tired from the trip? I thought you would never get here!"

The others gathered around, and soon they were all laughing, making jokes, and catching up on the news. As dusk began to fall, Teofila reminded them that they would need to make plans for the night. The Shining Path preferred darkness to enhance the element of surprise.

Margarita Fajardo slipped out the door with a friend who had come along for the trip. "Let's sit out on the porch so we won't bother anyone." As they settled onto a bench, they were startled by a loud BOOM! They looked down the valley from where they thought the explosion had come, but they couldn't see anything. *That was close*, Margarita thought to herself. Then the sound of another explosion came booming down from somewhere on the mountain above them. "It's a signal, I'm sure of it," she told her friend.

But was it the military, or was it the Shining Path? As she was trying to make up her mind whether to warn the others, Rómulo slipped out of the house. He had his hat on and a small backpack over his shoulder.

"Where are you headed at this hour?" Margarita asked.

"I'm going out for a walk."

"But it's not safe to go out there now," Margarita said with alarm and told him about the two explosions. "You can't go out there, Rómulo. It's too late! How could you even consider it? Can't you wait until morning?"

Laughing, Rómulo said, "Woman, this is my town. Don't worry."

Margarita shook her head. "Rómulo, have you been gone too long? The Shining Path is everywhere. Why risk it?" She defiantly stood in his way.

"Well, all right," he relented. "If you feel that strongly about it, I can wait until morning."

As the evening wore on, Rómulo's optimistic spirit seemed to flag. The cold mountain chill drifted through the room, and he felt vulnerable to the powers that controlled this part of the world. He began to sense the danger that the people of Chakiqpampa lived with day in and day out.

After dinner Rómulo called a family meeting. "Let's gather over there," he said motioning to a part of the house that had been damaged in a previous terrorist attack. It was no longer livable, but the large area would allow them all to comfortably gather together.

"Come," he called out. "We'll have a family meeting and pray."

Everyone shuffled in and looked to Rómulo for direction. "We need to spend some time praying together," he said. "Uncle Arcangel, you thank the Lord for our safe arrival. And, Margarita, you pray for whatever you'd like, and we'll follow in agreement."

Margarita did a double take. *Why have I been chosen?* she thought. *Usually they choose men to pray, and they're very specific about what they should pray for.*

When it was Margarita's turn, she prayed, "Lord, we're Your children. Your Word says that those who are encamped around us are greater than those who oppose us. In the name of Jesus, send Your angels to surround us with Your love. We ask this in the precious name of Jesus. Amen."

After prayers the family began to discuss sleeping arrangements. Teofila gathered her things and headed off for the caves. She hadn't slept in her own house in quite some time. After her husband's death, she didn't feel safe in Chakiqpampa at night. In fact, most of the villagers—the majority of them Christians—would already be at the caves when she arrived. Chakiqpampa was a marked village. The rebels knew they would never make any inroads there. No one cared about their ideology and their ruthless methods to coerce people to join their cause.

While some family members decided to join Teofila in the caves, Rómulo and a few others decided to sleep in a nearby hut. The rebels wouldn't think to look there. It wasn't really a house—just a place to store things. As the others prepared to leave, Rómulo called out to Marco Antonio, one of his nephews, "Marco, why don't you come with me? It's not safe to stay in the house. Anything could happen."

Marco held back. "I don't think so, Uncle Rómulo. I'd rather stay here with Uncle Arcangel."

Arcangel was pleased. "Good, I could use the company."

"Well, Marco, it's up to you," Rómulo said. "But I think it's too dangerous." He turned and headed off to the hut with the others.

After several hours, the dogs began bark. The sound roused everybody, and they came running.

"Hello!" a man called out in the darkness. They strained to see who it could be. Then a group of men came up carrying heavy backpacks Rómulo recognized as some of the supplies they had shopped for earlier that day. Others were carrying instruments. It was Alfredo Fajardo! He had brought the musicians for the big memorial celebration Rómulo had planned in honor of Grandfather Justiniano.

Margarita cried, "Oh, Alfredo, I was so worried." And she flung her arms around him.

By now Teofila had made her way down to the house, her heart pounding with fear. When she saw it was Alfredo, she lectured him, "You've put us all in danger by coming here so late in the night, Alfredo. You don't come into our village at this hour unless you're bringing trouble. You should have waited until first light." She turned on her heels and headed back to her hiding place.

Rómulo looked at the sheepish Alfredo and laughed. "I'm glad you came, Alfredo. You're just like me. If you say you're going to do something, you do it, no matter what. Come on, I'll show you where you can rest for the night." As they headed off to bed, Rómulo said to his friend, "Tomorrow I'm going to show you the places from my childhood. Our time here will be an unforgettable adventure." He held up the video camera. "Look, we're making something historical. The Lord is going to do marvelous things. We're going to turn the crisis of our people into great progress."

As the family ate breakfast the following morning, Rómulo whipped everyone into a frenzy of excitement. "We've got to get going. Think of all the people we're going to see. I want to make sure we don't miss any of the special places where we used to go when we were children," he chattered. Soon they were off down the trail. As they headed toward their old schoolhouse, they ran into Ezekiel, one of their childhood classmates. "Oh, Ezekiel, what a surprise to run into you!" Rómulo said warmly. "I thought you'd be off somewhere in the city by now."

"No, no," Ezekiel shook his head. "I still live around here. If you want, I can show you around. A lot has changed here in the past few years."

"Great!" Rómulo said. "And by the way, you should know our visit here is special because we're reliving the past. And when we get back to the house, we're going to have a big celebration in honor of my grandfather. Will you come?" Turning to the others, Rómulo grinned and said, "When we get back we're going to eat, we're going to play volleyball, and no one is going to be sad! That's an order."

They were soon at the little schoolhouse where Rómulo had repeated first grade two times. "Let's see if we can go inside," Rómulo suggested impulsively. "Hey, look at this," he pointed out. "Remember this . . ." and he went on, "How about the time we . . ." Two teachers came out of a classroom to see what was going on.

"Hello," Rómulo said, and began explaining the reason for their visit. "We're originally from Chakiqpampa, and some of us used to go to school here." Then he launched off on a long description of his childhood and what had happened to the family since then. "We're having a big celebration this afternoon in honor of my grandfather. Will you come?" he said without even thinking about the fact that the teachers were complete strangers.

As they walked on down the trail, Arcangel chided Rómulo. "You shouldn't be so open about your plans and the reason for your visit. The eyes and the ears of the Shining Path are everywhere! You have to be careful with strangers, Rómulo."

Rómulo gave his uncle a friendly punch. "You worry too much, Uncle."

Soon they came up to the edge of a deep ravine. At the bottom was a rushing stream.

"See that water down there? That's where I used to go to fetch water first thing every morning. I used to be able to scamper down and back in minutes. Let's go down," Rómulo said excitedly. "Ruben, you can tape this to show how we used to do it long ago."

As they climbed down the rugged terrain, they reached a smooth rock that stood about two feet high. "Hey, what's this?" Rómulo exclaimed. "This rock has shrunk. When I was a kid, I used to think it was a big boulder. Why, we used to slide down the side over here." He pointed to a gentle grade down the back side. "I guess I must have grown," he said with a shrug, and they were on their way again.

As they climbed out of the ravine, Arcangel pointed to a rocky section of the trail ahead. "Hey, Rómulo, remember when one of our lambs got his leg stuck in the rocks over there?"

"How could I forget?"

"I don't remember how we got him out, do you?"

"Sure, we greased his leg with some pig fat, and it popped right out," Rómulo said with a laugh.

It seemed that at every landmark there was a story to tell. Rómulo could hardly contain his joy, and he breathed a prayer of thanksgiving, "Oh, Lord, I've dreamed about coming home for so long. Thank you for allowing this dream to come true."

Back at the village, the women were busy preparing the *pachamanca.* As the men returned from their trek, they could hear the musicians tuning up and practicing a few songs. But Rómulo's heart was beginning to grow heavy. After the *pachamanca,* they would go to his grandfather's grave. The thought of coming face to face with the reality of his grandfather's brutal death made him sad.

"Come on, Rómulo," Margarita called out. "The *pachamanca* is ready!"

They crowded around the feast. Rómulo knew the women had been working for hours on its preparation. First they marinated the lamb meat they had brought with them. Then the women built a fire in a stone-lined pit, and the stones were heated until they were red hot. They removed all the charred wood and coals and laid the enormous chunks of meat right on top of the stones. Herbs and spices were sprinkled on top, with a good helping of potatoes, ground corn wrapped in leaves, and *habas* or lima beans. Then they covered it with a layer of dirt and left it for about an hour—like a giant pressure cooker.

The wait was worth it! The women heaped plates full of meat and potatoes and beans, and then dripped a delicious dressing of herbs and spices over the top. Everyone was delighted with the celebration. It had been a long time since the Quicañas had hosted such an event. As usual, Rómulo scanned the crowd to make sure everyone had been served.

Rómulo thought about all of his experiences since leaving Chakiqpampa. How could he have ever imagined as a child traveling the world and meeting so many interesting people. But even as he went beyond the borders of his country, he never failed to take the story of the suffering of his beloved Quechua people to the rest of the world.

One of Rómulo's great joys was introducing people to the Quechuas of Peru—especially at this time of suffering when they desperately needed prayer. In January 1990 a young man arrived in Lima for a research visit. Richard Luna's ministry was to reach out to the suffering church wherever it might be and provide it with Bibles, literature, and spiritual encouragement. He decided to visit Peru and see how his ministry, Open Doors with Brother Andrew, could help the church there.

As he began to call on the leadership of the Peruvian church, he found out about TAWA, the indigenous Quechua mission. So he called the leader, Rómulo Sauñe, and explained his mission. "If it's possible, I'd really like to go up to Ayacucho and see what is happening and how we can help. Would you be willing to go with me?"

Rómulo was silent for a moment. "Brother, what church are you with?"

"I'm not with one particular church, Rómulo. I work with an

interdenominational ministry that helps everyone who needs and wants our assistance."

"Great! I'm so tired of people who want to focus on only this church or that church. It's better to work with the whole body of believers," Rómulo said. After a short pause, he asked, "Are you aware how dangerous a place Ayacucho is to work in? Are you sure you want to go?" And he explained what had happened to his grandfather.

As Richard heard Rómulo's story, he knew his mission had to help the Quechua church. "Our mission has a calling to reach out to the suffering church and be sure that everyone has access to the Word of God."

"Then we definitely have to take you to Ayacucho," Rómulo said.

Months later they were able to synchronize their schedules, and they were off to Ayacucho. The two bonded like brothers. For Rómulo it was the first time someone had come to the Quechuas from the outside and asked, "How can we serve you?" Understandably, the foreign missionaries had left Ayacucho when the terrorism threatened their lives. But still the believers were lonely for someone to care for them, to stand with them in their trials and their anguish.

Together, Romulo and Richard planned a strategy of sending out teams to encourage and offer spiritual nurture. Young Quechua men would load up Bibles in their backpacks and hike into the mountains to visit Christian families. Others would pack in film projectors, video playback equipment, and generators to screen the movie *Jesus,* which made the Gospels come alive to the people. With the help of Open Doors, many churches received courage to carry on.

Richard Luna also introduced Rómulo to global organizations that could help in areas Open Doors was not equipped to handle. They promised to work side by side with Rómulo and TAWA to implement desperately needed medical and food relief programs.

Rómulo's network of contacts began to expand as never before. Soon invitations to speak arrived in the mail from Alaska, Mexico, Israel, the Philippines, Argentina, and many other places he had never visited before. In late 1991 the Billy Graham crusade in Argentina invited Rómulo to help coordinate continentwide broadcasts. He was the voice of Billy Graham in Quechua to his people scattered throughout the Andes. It was an exciting time for Rómulo, as well as for the members of TAWA.

For the Sauñes 1992 was supposed to be a year of rest in the United States. But Rómulo was busier than ever. With the family safely settled in Atlanta near Donna's parents, Rómulo began to accept invitations to travel and speak throughout the United States and abroad. On a trip to California he met with Richard Luna of Open Doors to review their accomplishments and make plans for the future.

While visiting with Richard, Rómulo received a phone call from the World Evangelical Fellowship. "We will be honoring a representative of the suffering church at our next world meetings," the representative explained. "Should you be chosen, would you accept such international recognition? Would this harm your ministry in any way?"

Rómulo talked it over with Richard.

"I think it's very possible that you will be chosen, Rómulo."

Rómulo's eyes filled with tears. He told Richard, "If I accept, it will be on behalf of all my Quechua brothers and sisters who have suffered for the sake of the gospel. I can't accept it just for myself." His heart filled with joy at the prospect of the chance to tell believers worldwide about his people's suffering.

Rómulo couldn't remember a time when the Christian world had honored a native American over a *mestizo*. In Latin America all the accolades went to the Spanish leaders, never to the indigenous leaders. Rómulo told Richard about a German who had received a prestigious award for discovering a plant with important medicinal properties. "We've known about this plant for centuries, but it was an outsider who was recognized with an award."

From March to June, however, a controversy arose in Peru over Rómulo's selection. Some Spanish church leaders felt that the recognition should go to someone more prominent. Rómulo was perhaps the unwitting victim of a natural bias that has always existed in Latin culture—a bias that causes the spotlight to fall on Latin *mestizos* rather than members of native cultures, who are often relegated to the social and political fringe.

But in searching for a candidate, the World Evangelical Fellowship had looked for someone who had served Christ in the midst of unspeakable hardship and persecution, whose testimony would inspire the church around the world. There was no doubt in the minds of the awards committee—Rómulo fit the profile.

This controversy deeply wounded Rómulo. For a man who had risked his life to translate the Word of God for his people, who had lost relatives in the conflict, whose grandfather and mentor had been brutally murdered, whose family home had been burned down at least two times, whose home church had been demolished, whose grandmother had been raped and brutalized—all for the sake of Christ, it seemed unbelievable that anyone would question his selection.

In June when Rómulo arrived in Manila, Philippines, to receive the award, he was checking in at the hotel's front desk when a Peruvian church leader came up to him. "Rómulo, what are you doing here?" the man asked loudly.

"Brother, I was invited," Rómulo said, startled.

"Rómulo, you don't deserve this award, and you shouldn't be here." He abruptly turned and walked away.

Rómulo was crushed. Old feelings surfaced, feelings he had had years ago when he had arrived in Ayacucho and found himself amidst the Spanish culture. *Who am I, a Quechua shepherd boy, to be here in the midst of all this privilege? Perhaps a* mestizo *should be getting this award.* But ever the optimist, Rómulo put on a courageous smile and shrugged off the incident. God had made it possible for him to receive this recognition, and he would not dishonor the Lord by moping about.

The award ceremony took place in a large hall in the Manila Hyatt Regency. Representatives of the evangelical church from around the world packed the auditorium. Rómulo stepped to the podium in his richly ornamented poncho and Peruvian highland hat to accept the award. ". . . I receive it not for myself, but in the name of my Quechua people, descendants of the great Inca Empire, who are caught in the cross-fire of political strife and injustice in the country of Peru."

The audience listened with rapt attention. Many from Africa, Asia, Europe, the Middle East, Latin America, and North America were hearing for the first time about the struggles of the Peruvian church.

"I receive this honor in memory of those who have striven to take the peace and love of our Lord Jesus and have died for their faith—leaders, pastors, missionaries, brothers and sisters in Christ, and my own grandfather who died serving God. Also I receive this honor in the name of Quechua widows and orphans, raped women and children, the unjustly accused brothers and sisters, the mutilated and the lame. . . . I thank God for raising up Quechua leaders who are proud of being Quechua in these difficult times. Those who brought the gospel from afar have had to retreat, but their fruit, native leaders, continue to take the good news of Jesus Christ. Most of these leaders work without salary, walking days to reach distant villages with the gospel. We have experienced firsthand that where there is suffering there are open hearts and great harvest. . . ."

He picked up his Quechua flute and began to play the tune he had composed for Psalm 23. As the last notes rang out across the audience, the delegates broke into loud applause, some wiping tears from their eyes. Rómulo's characteristic smile beamed across the room, and his heart pounded with joy. *Finally,* he thought, *the world knows that the Quechua church, despite its sufferings, is living triumphantly for the Lord and His Kingdom.*

14

Home

It was hard for Rómulo to relax. Was everyone enjoying the *pachamanca?* Was anyone left out? Did they have enough? Would Grandfather have done it differently?

"Here, Rómulo," Margarita came over with a plate of barbecued lamb. "It's your turn to eat, so stop worrying about everyone else. They've all been served." She knew Rómulo well.

After they had played a few rounds of volleyball, Rómulo called out, "It's time to go to the cemetery. We're going to hold a memorial service for Grandfather Justiniano."

As the group began to walk the short distance to the cemetery, Rómulo dashed back to his grandmother's house to pick up what was left of the silk flower bouquet he had brought for Grandfather's grave. Where was the box he had put it in? He had left it over in the corner with his things. But now it was nowhere in sight. A wave of disappointment came over him. Not again. Someone must have taken it. The temptation of the pretty flowers was too much. Tears began to stream down his cheeks. The one critical item he had guarded so carefully on his trip down from the States was now gone. For years he had planned to lay these flowers on his grandfather's grave.

Margarita came looking for him. As she approached Teofila's

house, she spied him in the garden picking flowers. When he turned toward her, she saw the tears.

"Rómulo, why are you crying?" she asked, giving him a hug.

"Oh, Margie," he said, "someone has taken the flowers I brought for my grandfather. I'm so hurt that someone would do such a thing. Nothing is safe even in my grandfather's house!"

Margarita helped him pick a handful of flowers from Teofila's garden, and together they walked toward the cemetery in silence.

On the way down they met Arcangel. "Rómulo, I can't go with you." He had never visited the grave. And now waves of grief were washing over him. He had been away studying in Brazil when his father was murdered. There had never been a chance to say farewell to the old man.

"What's wrong, Arcangel? What are you saying?" Rómulo asked kindly, forgetting his own grief for a moment.

"Rómulo, in my mind it's been like my father was away on a long trip. If I go into the cemetery and see his grave, it will cement in my mind that he's gone forever. I just don't think I can do this."

Rómulo looked at his dear friend with compassion. "Arcangel," he said firmly, "you're not only going to go into that cemetery, but you're going to lead the way."

There was no use arguing with Rómulo. Arcangel turned and made his way through the crowd waiting outside the cemetery. With a heavy heart he lifted the bar and swung open the wooden gate. Everyone streamed in after him and gathered around Justiniano Quicaña's grave.

Rómulo made his way to a little rise nearby and began to read a passage from the Gospel of Mark: "Whoever wants to become great among you must be your servant, and whoever wants to be first must be slave of all. For even the Son of Man did not come to be served, but to serve, and to give his life as a ransom for many."

He lifted his eyes and smiled, pausing to look from relative to friend, from friend to neighbor. "Our Lord came to serve, not to

be served. You all knew my grandfather. He preached the gospel
for many years here and in many other places. Many of us first
heard the gospel sitting at his feet. He dedicated his life to his people and to the preaching of the gospel. One day when the Lord
returns, He will lift Grandfather Justiniano's body out of this
grave and take it to Glory.

"Life is fleeting, but one day we will be together in Heaven
with our Heavenly Father. Until then, like my grandfather, I want
to serve my people. I have not come to you to be served, but to
work side by side with you that the gospel might be preached and
the Word of our Lord be known everywhere we go. I love you all
very much."

Then turning tear-filled eyes toward heaven he said,
"Grandfather, when you were alive here in Chakiqpampa, you
put on great banquets for the whole village, and then you would
preach the gospel." Rómulo wept as he continued. "I've come to
do the same thing now, Grandfather. And I know that you're
happy that we have carried on your work. Now you're in the
presence of the Lord, Grandfather. And you're all dressed in
white. I'm envious of you that you are there and I am here. . . ."
He began to sob. Tears flowed down people's faces as they
remembered Justiniano, their friend, teacher, and brother in the
Lord.

The group quietly filed out of the cemetery and headed up the
winding path to the Chakiqpampa church founded by old
Justiniano. As they took their places, they looked to Rómulo,
expecting him to preach. But Rómulo sat in the back and
remained quiet.

Enrique Sauñe walked up to the podium and invited the musicians to lead them in worship. Everyone who had a Bible took it
out, and they began singing Scripture. Most of the Quechua
hymns were taken straight from the text, and everyone knew the
tunes by heart. As they sang, Rómulo's thoughts drifted back to
the cemetery. The work was done. He had honored his grandfa-

ther's memory as he had promised himself to do when Justiniano was so brutally torn from the earth.

Enrique began to preach. A dynamic speaker, he knew just how to bring encouragement to this little flock. After all, that was the reason for venturing out on this perilous journey. As he finished speaking and stepped down, Rómulo approached the front.

"One day we will all wear white robes," he began haltingly. "If I don't have another opportunity to come back and visit you, remember that we will all be together in Heaven. So don't cry." Some in the audience were weeping. His heart filled with compassion for these isolated and suffering Quechua brethren. He knew that every family in the church had lost a loved one. So had he. And that knowledge bound them together.

"The Lord is with us, brothers and sisters," Rómulo continued. "Here is Alfredo, and here is Arcangel, and here are some of the other brothers whom I will send to you. They will bring you the things you need. Don't worry! Just keep following the Lord. Don't ever leave Him. There will be times when you'll feel like giving up, but please don't. I want us to be together once again in Heaven. There we will be like one big family."

Then Rómulo opened his Bible and began sharing his dreams with the people. As he spoke the words of Scripture about the glories of Heaven and all that the Lord had prepared for them, the sadness he had felt moments earlier began to dissipate.

"Now bring the little children forward," he said, as he closed his Bible. When the children were lined up at the front, Rómulo reached for a large bag of candy and began handing it out. Ecstatic, the children squealed with excitement.

Then Rómulo called the widows of the village to come forward. Their lives had always been characterized by poverty, but now alone they barely eked out a living working their fields and coping with their loneliness.

"Brothers and sisters, my intention was to bring everyone a gift from my trip abroad. Many of the things I was bringing you were lost along the way. So please forgive me for the little I've brought. But what is here you are welcome to have." He began to distribute the clothing and other items.

Then Ruben and Alfredo set up a video monitor, and everyone gathered around to view a film. Alfredo fired up the generator. As the image of Christ came onto the screen and began to speak, someone yelled out, "That's Rómulo!" When the Quechua version of the *Jesus* film had been dubbed, Rómulo had been recruited to do the voice of Christ. Everyone smiled and laughed. When the film was over, the people begged to watch it over and over.

Dawn peeked over the horizon, Saturday, September 5, but Rómulo had already been up praying for several hours. After a small breakfast, he called out to his family, "I'll be back later. I want to go see someone."

Gripping his Quechua Bible, he went to visit a family that had failed to show up for yesterday's festivities. By midmorning, Rómulo was back in Chakiqpampa with the head of the household he had gone to visit. He was so excited he seemed to float into the house. "Everyone! Gather around. This man and his entire family came to Christ today," he beamed. "I led them to the Lord, and now they're a part of God's family. Congratulate them and welcome them into the family of God." One by one, the Quicañas and the Sauñes came up and shook the man's hand, giving him warm hugs and wishing him God's blessings.

Soon it was time for everyone to say good-bye to Teofila and begin the journey back to Ayacucho. As the others finished packing, Rómulo approached his grandmother.

"Grandmother, I'll be praying for you every day that we're apart, that God will protect you and give you strength. Thank you for this wonderful visit. It's been a blessing to be here with you these few days."

"Yes, Rómulo. Thank you so much for coming. Now when will you be coming back?" Grandmother Teofila asked hopefully.

Rómulo would always give her a specific date. But this time, he only smiled and promised, "Don't worry. I'll be back soon. You'll see."

Then they were off down the trail. Rómulo turned to give his grandmother a final wave. But Arcangel hung back from the others for a moment to have a private word with his mother.

"Mother, please take care of yourself. If you need anything at all, don't hesitate to let Fernando know, and he will get in touch with me right away." His brother Fernando lived closer to Teofila and often checked on her.

"Oh, Arca, don't worry about me. I'm just an old woman. My times are in God's hands and care," she said with a smile. "Now you go with God's blessing and be careful."

With a final hug, Arcangel left to catch up with the others who had stopped to say good-bye to a neighboring Christian family. Rómulo wanted to pray with them before he left Chakiqpampa. "Father, You know the needs of these people. Touch them and care for them in a way that only You can with Your mighty power. Amen."

The neighbor gave Rómulo a thankful smile. "Brother Rómulo, we want to give you something. Please take this new little lamb from our flock. It will remind you of your days as a shepherd and the love of our Good Shepherd, Jesus."

Rómulo protested at first. The family was practically destitute. But when he saw the man's sincerity, he thanked him, "Brother, this is a gift I will always cherish."

Then he handed the lamb to his nephew Marco Antonio. The teenager flipped the lamb onto his shoulders and headed off down the trail.

As they walked into Paccha where Arcangel and Alfredo had stored their vehicles, a group of believers gathered around. Arcangel thought, *Here we go again. We'll be here for hours while Rómulo visits with all the people.* He was anxious to get back to Ayacucho, but this was Rómulo's trip, and he didn't want to interfere. Instead he decided to take a little nap on the grass by the parked pickup.

The people had been waiting anxiously for Rómulo to come back through Paccha. As Rómulo listened to their concerns, one man asked, "Rómulo, is there any way you could get me a Quechua Bible?"

"Sure, brother, that won't be a problem," and he asked him for his address. Then he turned to Margarita. "Could you take down the names of anyone who needs a Bible?"

Rómulo then left the group in Margarita's care and went looking for Arcangel. "Hey, Arcangel," he said when he caught up with him over by the pickup. "We've got to get going, Uncle. It's getting late." Arca was surprised, but pleased.

Suddenly, Arca's sister Priscila who was in Paccha, approached him. "Arca, could we get a ride back with you to Ayacucho?" She stood there with her boyfriend, a policeman. Arca hesitated. He didn't want her to think he approved of her live-in arrangement with an unsaved man. But still he felt obligated to at least give his sister a ride.

"Well? Can we go with you or not?" Priscila asked again.

Arcangel turned to Margarita who had ridden with him on the trip in. "How are you getting back, Margarita? Are you going to ride with your husband?"

"Yes. Don't worry about us."

Turning back to Priscila, Arcangel reluctantly said, "There's room now if you want to come with me."

Then he called out to the others, "Let's get going!"

Everyone piled into the pickup. As Arcangel slowly pulled out onto the highway, two strangers grabbed on to the back and pulled themselves aboard. Everyone in the back courteously made room for them, thinking they had made previous arrangements with Arcangel for a ride into Ayacucho.

About an hour later, as they rounded a curve and approached a crossroads, the passengers in the back began banging on the cab. "Stop! Stop! Someone wants to get off!"

Arcangel braked and pulled over to the side of the road. As far as he knew, everyone was going to Ayacucho. He heard someone jump off the back and walk up to the driver's side window.

"How much do I owe you for the ride?" asked the stranger.

Surprised, Arcangel stammered, "Half a *sol*."

"I've only got a one-*sol* bill."

Arcangel shrugged. He was still trying to figure out how the man had gotten on board.

"Oh, just keep it," the stranger said and walked away.

Arcangel pulled back onto the highway. He would talk to the others about it when they reached the Arizona Restaurant, their usual rest stop and an oasis for travelers on this lonely stretch of the road.

As they sat at one of the tables, Arcangel kept his silence. He was trying to understand why the stranger had sneaked onto his truck and then gotten off at such a remote place. There was no town, no village. There was only a footpath leading over the hills toward Ayacucho.

Rómulo was talking to Priscila and her boyfriend. "The Bible says that one day each of us will have to give an accounting of our lives to the Lord Jesus Christ. We can't gain salvation by our works—it's only because of the sacrifice of God's Son on the cross that we can be blameless before Him."

The policeman stared at Rómulo. "You sound like you believe what you're talking about. Death is common in my line of work.

It would be good to know that I'm going to Heaven when I die. But I'm just not ready to make a decision."

Rómulo just smiled and kept right on speaking. There might not be another chance.

Meanwhile, Miguel, Arcangel's son, was pestering him for a coke. "Dad, can you buy me a soda?" Arcangel didn't respond. "Come on, Dad, I want a coke or a Seven-up. Please? Please?" Miguel's badgering irritated him like scratching fingernails across a blackboard.

"I don't have any money for that," Arcangel chided.

The boy turned away, stung by the rebuke.

Suddenly, Rómulo went up to the counter. "Two cokes, please."

With the straws floating out of the top of the bottles, Rómulo set the sodas down in front of Arcangel and Miguel. "Here, my gift to both of you." And he winked at Miguel.

Arcangel thought, *That's just like Rómulo, always looking out for everyone else.* But his mind was still on the stranger. Then out of the corner of his eye he spied another stranger lingering by the truck. *If he is from another vehicle, why is he paying so much attention to mine?* thought Arcangel.

"Hey," he called over to his nephew Josué, "do you know who that guy is?" He pointed out the window.

Josué glanced over. "Oh, that guy is riding with us. Didn't you offer him a ride?"

"I've never seen him before."

Rómulo caught the conversation and looked out also. Arcangel asked, "Have you ever seen him, Rómulo?"

Rómulo shook his head, but said nothing. Arcangel thought he looked troubled. "What is it?" he asked. Again, Rómulo shook his head and turned away. In these uncertain times, one didn't pick up strangers without taking a great risk. Arcangel felt compromised. And he was angry at the others for not having told him about the extra two passengers.

Soon they were back on the highway. Rómulo didn't join in the chatter. It was as though a cloud had come over him. Arcangel assumed he was saddened at leaving Chakiqpampa. Perhaps the mountains were calling the shepherd boy home. Perhaps he could hear in his mind the sound of a gentle flute coloring the air with sound.

Suddenly, the pickup's engine began to sputter. With a final jerk, the engine stalled, and the vehicle came to a standstill.

"What a place to break down," Arcangel muttered as he tried to get the pickup going again. "Something must be blocking the fuel line."

Rómulo nodded, but remained silent. Then the engine roared to life, and Arcangel eased the truck back onto the highway. Minutes later he slowed down to turn a sharp curve, and he gasped. Everyone looked up.

"A roadblock!" they cried out in unison. There was a collection of some twenty-five cars, buses, and trucks stopped in a line.

"It's the Shining Path," Arcangel said quietly. "What should we do now?" At first he thought about backing up and heading back down the highway, but if there were any rebel lookouts, they would certainly shoot him for the suspicious move. No, they were trapped.

One of the gunmen walked up the road toward the pickup and motioned to Arcangel to come forward. He wasn't masked, Arcangel thought with relief. Perhaps it was just the local civil patrol checking identification papers. But he was troubled about being singled out of the lineup.

As he inched the pickup up to the roadblock itself, he noticed three other gunmen and a woman—they were masked! It was a Shining Path barrier. He spotted more and more rebels. It seemed like at least 100! Alarmed, Arcangel stopped and climbed out of the cab. Enrique followed him and in an attempt to calm everyone's fears, he called back to the passengers, "It's the police."

At the word *police* the gunmen panicked. "What police!"

They surrounded Arcangel, Enrique, and the pickup. "Get out!" they ordered the passengers. "Now! Everyone out!" Rómulo and the rest scrambled out of the car.

"Women over there!" one of the gunmen commanded pointing to the side of the road. "You too!" he shouted at Enrique. But Enrique refused to move. He wanted to stay with the other men. Arcangel shoved him. "Go on, get out of the way." Enrique reluctantly stumbled off.

"You men, line up in front of the pickup," the gunman ordered, firing his weapon in the air. Alarmed, Rómulo, Arcangel, Marco Antonio, Josué, and Priscila's boyfriend lined up. The stranger from Paccha had disappeared.

"Give me the gasoline out of your truck," one of the gunmen ordered Arcangel.

"Here are the keys to the gas tank," Arcangel said, "but you can't get the gasoline out. It has a safety device that won't allow it. But you're welcome to try, if you want."

"You just don't want to give us your gasoline," the gunman said.

"No, that's not true. If I could give it to you, I would. Go ahead and try yourself."

Pop! Pop! Pop! It sounded like firecrackers. The gunman turned to see what was happening down the road. The guerrillas were ordering passengers off a bus. A panic-stricken woman was stuck trying to get out through a window. "Oh my God, oh my God, I can't get out!" she cried as someone reached to help.

A guerrilla screamed impatiently, "I said get out of the bus now!"

The woman was hopelessly wedged in. "Please, don't shoot; please, don't shoot," she pleaded. But the guerrilla was in no mood to wait. He raised his weapon and shot her in the head. The woman slumped over hanging halfway out the window. Stunned, the passengers tripped and stumbled over each other to get out before more shots were fired. One man tried to make a run for it across the adjacent field. Another guerrilla raised his rifle and took aim. Bang! The man crumpled to the ground with a jerk.

"No! No! No!" shouted his friend, and he began to scream in terror. "Don't shoot! Don't shoot! Stop it, stop it!" he sobbed. The guerrilla turned and fired. The sobs were silenced.

Suddenly, one of the gunmen who was going through Arcangel's truck shouted, "I found a pistol!"

His companion walked up to the Sauñe-Quicaña passengers. "Whose gun is this?"

Everyone looked at the ground. No one said a word.

"I said whose gun is this?" the gunman shouted.

Arcangel's heart sank. He thought it belonged to Marco Antonio. He recalled that back in Chakiqpampa, Miguel, his son, had asked if he and Marco Antonio could have permission to shoot at the ducks down at the pond.

Now Arcangel was in a panic. He edged over to Marco Antonio and scolded him under his breath, "Why did you bring the gun with you? Why didn't you tell me?"

"I don't know what you're talking about," Marco retorted. "I don't have a gun. Besides, look, it's a police-issue pistol. I've never owned anything like that."

Arcangel saw that it was true. Then one of the gunmen shouted at Arcangel, "Where did you pick up the miserable policeman?"

"What policeman?" Arcangel said as innocently as he could. "We didn't pick up anyone. We're a family traveling together."

The gunmen glared at the men. "Where are you coming from?"

"From Paccha."

"Which way did you drive to get from Paccha to here?"

"We went through Vinchos."

"Did you see any police in Vinchos?"

"Yes."

"How many?"

"I don't know, but there is a police station in that town."

"I think you picked up a policeman there, and he's one of you."

"No, I didn't."

"You're lying," the guerrilla sneered. "We've got a police pistol here from a sleeping bag we found in your truck. Explain that!" He raised his gun and pointed it at Arcangel.

Terrified, Miguel threw himself on the man. "Don't kill my father!" he screamed.

"Get out of the way." The terrorist shoved him off.

Miguel stumbled to the ground, then scrambled up, and stood in front of his father. "Don't kill my father," he pled. Arcangel gripped his shoulders and tried to push him behind. The guerrilla lowered his gun and decided not to shoot.

By now Enrique was tired of waiting with the women. He returned to the lineup of men, hoping to protect them in some way.

What Rómulo and Arcangel didn't know was that when they had first seen the roadblock, Priscila's policeman boyfriend had taken out his concealed pistol and stuffed it into one of the sleeping bags.

The guerrillas moved away from the group for a moment, and the policeman standing next to Rómulo begged him, "Please, don't turn me in, Rómulo."

Rómulo just shook his head. He would never turn anyone in.

One of the gunmen then turned back to the group. "Who owns this sleeping bag?" He held up the bag in which the pistol had been found.

Arcangel stepped forward. "It's mine."

"You're lying."

"I am not," Arcangel replied. "That sleeping bag is mine, but I'm no policeman. I'm the driver of this pickup."

"Let's see your documents."

Arcangel pulled out his wallet and held out his driver's license.

"We're evangelicals. We're returning from a visit to Chakiq-pampa and Paccha." Had Arcangel known that the two villages were considered in rebellion against the Shining Path, he would have never mentioned it.

By now Rómulo and the others knew their fates were sealed. The guerrillas would never give up until they identified the police-man. And then they would be executed for concealing the fact. Rómulo bowed his head and began to pray silently, his hands clasped in front of him.

Arcangel tried to push Enrique away. "Get away while you can," he urged him.

Enrique resisted. "I want to die with my sons."

"Enrique, get out of here," Arcangel said giving him a stronger push.

"What are you doing?" the guerrilla snarled. "Stand at attention."

Enrique shuffled back to the knot of women a short distance away. They were trembling with fear.

One of the terrorists approached Ruben, Rómulo's youngest brother. He raised his gun and shot him in the chest at point blank range. Ruben, who had stood quietly, blurted out, "Jesus Christ!" and fell to the ground, dead.

Josué jumped forward and yelled, "I want to speak with you." He took two or three steps, but before he could say anything more, the guerrilla whipped around and cut him down with a single shot. With that the terrorists sprayed death from their machine guns at the remaining men. The Sauñe-Quicaña men fell to the ground like a set of dominoes.

"We got him!" one of the terrorists excitedly reported into his two-way radio, looking at Rómulo's body.

Arcangel had instinctively thrown himself to the ground when the bullets started to fly, and he had not been hit. His son Miguel, lying next to him, had not been hit either. Arcangel was weak with relief, but when he saw the pools of blood forming around the others, he screamed, "Why did you kill them? Is this what you want?" He threw his car keys at the guerrillas. The guerrilla turned and fired at Arcangel. Click! The chamber was empty. He turned back to his radio and listened for a reply. "Okay, that's enough. You can retreat now," the voice squawked back. The commander shouted to the others. "Retreat!" They began torching the vehicles. Suddenly, the thunder of a distant helicopter came drifting over the mountains. Moments later a military gunship helicopter began strafing the convoy of smoking vehicles. Everyone dove for cover. The guerrillas shot back from their hiding places, but they were no match for an armored helicopter.

As the commander who had shot the Sauñe-Quicaña men ran for cover, one of the helicopter's sharpshooters felled him with a single shot, and his chest exploded into a sea of red.

"Oh, Lord, save us," Arcangel cried out.

Then, just as suddenly as the helicopter had descended on the gruesome scene, it banked steeply and thundered off into the distance. The coast clear, rebels crawled out from their hiding places. With the discipline of highly trained commandos, they marched single file up into the hills where dozens more waited along the ridges.

Arcangel scooted out from under the pickup and ran to Rómulo and the others. He hoped they were only injured. But one look told him more than he wanted to know. Their ashen faces rested peacefully against the cold asphalt. Rómulo, Ruben, Josué, Marco Antonio, and the policeman—dead! As he turned away, he saw they weren't the only ones. On the highway, now a burning inferno, sprawled the bodies of more than twenty guerrillas and civilians. "When will the violence ever end?" he cried out. His body convulsed with grief.

them to some of Blake

self. They sang triumphantly

Epilogue

Tuesday morning the sky was a magnificent blue, and the sun quickly warmed the cool mountain air. People streamed from the mountains into Ayacucho and crowded into the El Arco church. Soon mourners filled every one of the eight hundred seats.

Outside, hundreds more stood in respectful silence around the church, hoping to hear just a bit of the service. Tears flowed freely. Many could remember moments when Rómulo had reached out to them with a kind word or a helping hand. But most knew him as the man who had brought God's Word to them in their own language and who had encouraged them to express their faith through their own traditions.

At the airport Arcangel watched the airplane from Lima land and taxi up to the terminal. The service had been in progress for more than an hour. Arcangel was amazed at Donna's strength. There were no tears welling up in her beautiful blue eyes. Instead he saw resolve, and this gave him courage.

The service was about over as they trooped to the front, and the people fell into a respectful silence. Already the pastor had led them in some of Rómulo's favorite hymns, many written by himself. They sang triumphantly, the words ringing out across the street and down the cobbled alleys of this troubled city Rómulo had loved so much.

Donna was invited to speak. As she stood before the four silver coffins flanked by iron candleholders, she recognized her husband's coffin by the copy of the Ayacucho Quechua Bible resting on the closed canopy. How many years they had labored together to bring God's Word to Rómulo's people. As she looked out at the sea of faces, her heart was filled with sadness and a bittersweet joy.

"When this happened," she began, her voice trembling and her eyes welling up with tears, "my first reaction was, 'God! Where were all Your angels?'" Tears flowed, but in a moment she regained composure. In a strong voice she recalled, "Rómulo often told me that he longed to be among his people when he died. We, the family, are thankful that Rómulo died in Ayacucho with his people and for our God. All of these were his life's purpose."

As the brethren began to line up in the streets for the five-mile walk to the cemetery, the leaders of the various denominations began to shuffle for the right to carry Rómulo's coffin. Finally they decided to take turns so everyone would have the privilege of ushering the fallen leader to his final resting place.

They moved into the street, and a Quechua Christian band led by TAWA's Julian Pareja struck up the familiar Quechua chords. Behind them churches lifted up banners proclaiming, "Ayacucho for Christ," and the verse, "For me to live is Christ, to die is gain."

The remaining members of the Sauñe-Quicaña clan linked arms. "Onward Christian soldiers . . . ," they sang, as the citizens of Ayacucho began lining the streets to pay their final respects. To them the procession seemed endless. There must have been over 2,000 people marching behind the family, all of them carrying their Bibles or placards and singing joyfully.

"Surely this must have been a great man," they commented

among themselves. Others who knew him simply stood there quietly with tears streaming down their faces. Ayacucho had never seen a funeral so triumphant.

When they finally arrived at the cemetery, the gates were locked and the caretakers gone for lunch. No one had thought to send a messenger ahead. But never mind, the celebration would continue. Gathering around, they lifted their voices in praise to the Lord. Then each family member gave a word of testimony.

Donna moved to the front at her turn and began to speak. "Brothers and sisters, today we are seeing Rómulo's vision become a reality. All my husband ever lived for was to see the uniting of all the Christians of Ayacucho, and he has now accomplished in his death what he could never do in his lifetime. He would have been so pleased." Then she urged the believers to remember what Rómulo had fought so hard for. "Don't be weary of doing good. Don't let divisions separate you. Work together, for this is the will of the Lord."

Perhaps Rómulo's uncle, Fernando Quicaña, summarized the moment best, later saying to friends, "Death is an ever-present reality for us. Any of us [Christian missionaries] face the same reality. Humanly speaking, this is very painful, but we have to trust in the sovereignty of God. Our lives are in His hands and in His will. As for us, we will continue to minister in the conflict areas. Please continue to pray for us, because as you can see, there is a very high cost."

Several days later back in Lima, seventy-year-old Enrique confided to a missionary, "I had hoped to retire and leave my ministry to my sons, but it looks like God still has work for me to do."

Though it cannot be said with certainty that God avenged Rómulo's death, the developments in the following week could hardly have been scripted better. Exactly one week after the massacre at the fateful roadblock, undercover agents from the National Counterterrorism Directorate gathered on a quiet street in the Surquillo suburb of Lima.

Several months previously a ballet instructor and an architect had rented a house. Strange clues began to come into the agents' hands. The ballerina had been buying sixteen bread rolls daily, and the trash contained discarded boxes of Winston cigarettes, a brand favored by Abimael Guzman. The mysterious leader of the Shining Path had gone underground more than twelve years ago, and he was the most wanted man in Peru. Agents put the house under surveillance.

One evening visitors began arriving at the house for a barbecue. Undercover agents rang the doorbell. When the door opened, they stormed in, securing the house with their drawn weapons. They found Guzman on the second floor with his companion, Elena Iparraguirre, the Shining Path's second in command. Seated at a table with a book in his hand, this paunchy, middle-aged man with thick glasses hardly looked the part of one who had loosed a reign of terror and chaos upon a whole country. Guzman calmly looked at the agents who had burst through the door.

"Bingo!" shouted an officer into his two-way radio. "We've got Big Cheeks."

Guzman glumly replied, "My turn to lose."

In October the government announced that the plotters of the September roadblock in which Rómulo had died had been captured and were being held in undisclosed locations around the country. Today its commander is turning state's evidence while awaiting trial in a Peruvian prison.

By December President Alberto Fujimori announced the capture of nearly 2,500 terrorists in a national roundup unprecedented in Peru's history.

Rómulo Sauñe's ministry continues today through the work of TAWA and the Scriptures he helped to translate into the language of his people. And the mountains ring with the music of their culture—a lasting tribute to a man who gave everything, even his life, that his people might know God and experience the fullness of His love for them.